WALKI.

NORTH Y
SOL

**Paul
Hannon**

HILLSIDE

For a full list of around 50 current *Hillside* titles,
please refer to the end of the book

WALKING COUNTRY

NORTH YORK MOORS
SOUTHERN

Paul Hannon

HILLSIDE

HILLSIDE
PUBLICATIONS
12 Broadlands
Shann Park
Keighley
West Yorkshire
BD20 6HX

First published in 1988 in different format.
Fully revised and extended 1995
5th impression 2004

ISBN 1 870141 30 X

Whilst the author has walked and researched all the routes for the purposes of this guide, no responsibility can be accepted for any unforeseen circumstances encountered while following them. The publisher would, however, greatly appreciate any information regarding material changes, and any problems encountered.

The sketch maps in this book are based upon
1925-1935 Ordnance Survey One-Inch maps

Printed in Great Britain by
Carnmor Print
95-97 London Road
Preston
Lancashire
PR1 4BA

CONTENTS

INTRODUCTION..6

THE WALKS

INTRODUCTION

THE NORTH YORK MOORS NATIONAL PARK

The North York Moors is the fourth largest of our National Parks, designated in 1952 with an area of 553 square miles. It is probably the best-defined upland area of all, rising island-like from the surrounding countryside. This creates an impression of much greater altitude than its very modest summit of 1490 feet attains. If asked which of the parks is bottom of the height table, few would be likely to provide the correct answer, the North York Moors.

On Rudland Rigg

To the north is the Cleveland Plain, westwards the Vales of Mowbray and York, and southwards the Vale of Pickering, while to the east is the ultimate low point, the North Sea. The Park itself however has a solid upland mass spreading from the centre towards the western escarpments, where one can walk for mile upon mile and lose little altitude. It is, of course, all this heather-clad moorland for which the North York Moors National Park is best known.

Heather moors, despite their profusion, are only one aspect of this diverse region, for here are some delightful green valleys and a spectacular length of coastline composed largely of rugged cliffs. There are sandy shorelines and rocky coves, and inland some shapely summits, fascinating rock outcrops, and beautiful waterfalls: and, despite all the forestry, some enchanting, indigenous woods. The hand of man appears to have been laid everywhere, even on the lonely moortops which are littered with ancient burial mounds and standing stones. The scores of villages range from fishing ports to moorland farming communities, though many of the villages are to be found beneath the hills, taking advantage of the shelter.

Man has also left ruined abbeys and castles; old roads including famous drovers' routes and Roman roads, and countless paved trods and packways going back to medieval times; absorbing relics of the former ironstone, alum and jet industries; and not least of all an unrivalled collection of wayside crosses, some being ancient christian symbols, and others serving as waymarks or boundary stones.

This is walkers' territory par excellence, with a plethora of long distance and challenge walks crossing it. Best known are the first, the Lyke Wake Walk, and the longest and best, the Cleveland Way, while the Coast to Coast Walk concludes here.

The Southern Moors

The subject of this volume is the southern area of the Park, which takes the form of a string of parallel but highly individual valleys running south from the high moors at the heart of the district. Further east the moors give way to softer environs, eventually becoming suffocated by the extensive forests. The major valleys are, from west to east, Bransdale (becoming Kirk Dale), Farndale, Rosedale, Newton Dale, Thornton Dale and the Derwent Valley (which includes the Forge Valley).

At Langdale End, featuring the Moorcock Inn and Methodist chapel

7

As the rivers and becks run off the moors, they encounter the other dominant feature of the area, namely the Tabular Hills. These crouching lions are ranged along the entire length of the southern moors, rising almost imperceptibly from the Vale of Pickering to then plunge sharply at the northern limit. Their table-top appearance - hence the name - means that one needs to be in the right place to appreciate their sleek profiles: this is usually either on the same latitude or to their north. Fortunately this is where most of the walks will be found.

The highest and shapeliest of these hills occupy the western half of the area, where the major dales narrow in order to break through into the flat vale. These Tabular Hills provide shelter for most of the villages in the district, though some are bravely perched on the plateaux. A regular feature of these communities is the long, wide main street, often with little other development, while some of the dale villages are graced with attractive becks flowing through their very centres.

Some of these villages are huge tourist draws, others are happy to retain their solitude. For every picture postcard view of Hutton-le-Hole and Thornton Dale, there are as many equally attractive scenes at places such as Gillamoor and Appleton-le-Moors.

Old kilns, Rosedale Chimney Bank Top

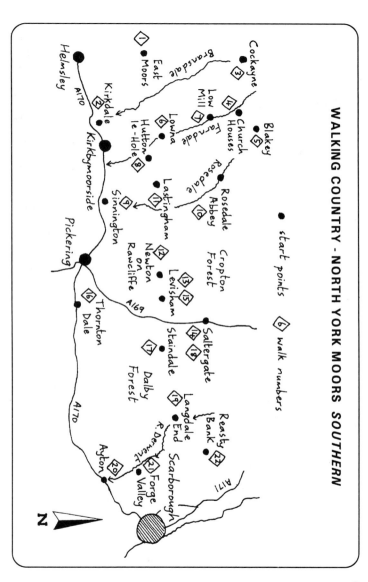

WALKING COUNTRY - NORTH YORK MOORS *SOUTHERN*

● start points

◇6 walk numbers

N

9

Getting around

Public transport to the area is good, and places along the main Helmsley-Scarborough road are well served. Many of the villages and dales, however, are at best infrequently served, some not at all. The area can also be reached by train to Scarborough. While only one of the walks is described as a linear ramble, any number of permutations can be created by linking different sections, and any opportunity to leave the car behind should be snatched with both hands. In addition to normal services, summer Sundays see the Moorsbus operating, which takes in villages such as Hutton-le-Hole and Rosedale Abbey.

Using the guide

Each walk is self-contained, with essential information being followed by a simple map and concise description of the route. Dovetailed between this are useful notes of features along the way, and interspersed are illustrations which both capture the flavour of the walks and document the many items of interest.

The sketch maps identify the location of the routes rather than the fine detail, and whilst the route description should be sufficient to guide one around, an Ordnance Survey map is recommended. The route as depicted can easily be plotted on the relevant OS map. To gain the most from a walk, the remarkable detail of the Outdoor Leisure maps cannot be matched: they also serve to vary walks as desired, giving an improved picture of one's surroundings and the availability of linking paths. This area is particularly fortunate in that two sheets give comprehensive coverage of the walks:

Sheet 26 - North York Moors, Western area
Sheet 27 - North York Moors, Eastern area

Also extremely useful for general planning purposes are the Landranger sheets, at 1:50,000. The following cover the area:
94 - Whitby   100 - Malton & Pickering
101 - Scarborough & Bridlington

In addition, the North York Moors 1-inch Tourist Map covers the whole area.

SOME USEFUL ADDRESSES

Ramblers' Association
2nd Floor, Camelford House, 87-89 Albert Embankment,
London SE1 7BR
Tel. 020-7339 8500

North York Moors National Park Information Service
The Old Vicarage, Bondgate, Helmsley, York YO6 5BP
Tel. 01439-770657

Tourist Information Centres

The Ropery, **Pickering** YO18 8DY   Tel. 01751-473791

Town Hall, Market Place, **Helmsley** YO62 5BL Tel. 01439-770173

Pavilion House, Valley Bridge Road, **Scarborough** YO11 1UZ
Tel 01723-373333

North Yorkshire Moors Association
Angulon House, Bank Lane, Faceby TS9 7BP
('friends of the moors' - a voice to protect the beauty of the area)

National Trust Regional Office
Goddards, 27 Tadcaster Road, York YO2 2QG
Tel. 01904-702021

Forestry Commission
Forest Enterprise, Outgang Road, Pickering YO18 7EL
Tel. 01751-472771

North Yorkshire Moors Railway
Pickering Station, Pickering, North Yorkshire YO18 7AJ
Tel. 01751-472508

Public transport information

Traveline   Tel. 0870-608 2608

National Rail Enquiry Line   Tel. 08457-484950

(1)

EAST MOORS

START   Carlton   Grid ref. SE 609903

DISTANCE 7 miles

ORDNANCE SURVEY MAPS
1:50,000
Landranger 100 - Malton & Pickering
1:25,000
Outdoor Leisure 26 - North York Moors (West)

ACCESS   Start from the isolated East Moors church, 2 ½ miles north of Carlton village on the Bransdale road (4 ½ miles north of Helmsley). There is ample verge parking opposite the church.

This, above all perhaps, is one for late summer. In many ways not a classic walk - though it gets you away from the crowds, for sure: but when the heather is ablaze and so is the sun, it's just wonderful.

Almost hidden in trees is the tiny church of St. Mary Magdalen, its additional protection being a lack of windows on its north side. It was built in 1882 to serve the scattered communities of East Moors, which then numbered little short of 200 souls. In 1898 it became part of Pockley cum East Moors parish, and is now administered from Helmsley. Today it is in a sorry plight, and in the latter years of its demise has seen use only on the feast of St. Mary Magdalen, and for the Harvest Festival. A faded notice tells of the times when the priest had to bed down in the south aisle because of bad weather on the moor - true sanctuary!

☐ **Take the footpath leaving the road by the phone box alongside the churchyard wall, through a small gate and straight on to a gate into a field.** From the outset of the walk, Birk Nab dominates a scene of all round loveliness, with bracken, pastures and woods

12

descending in stages to the beck. **Follow the left side of the field to a stile at the end, then go forward to Lund Farm's access road. Advance on it to a stile by a gate. When it turns down to the farm, continue a steady descent along the right side of several fields. At the bottom a path slants left through bracken to a gate in front of Bonfield Gill. The easiest crossing is by the stones just upstream.**

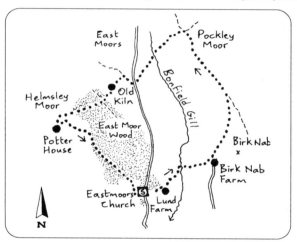

The next potential hazard will soon identify itself, for you'll quickly be aware if pigs are still in residence in the undergrowth. *They all ran away when I approached, but that may not mean a great deal!* **A sketchy track rises half-right to a wall, then rises with it to meet the surfaced road-end at Birk Nab Farm.** *The climb to this point promotes a glorious prospect of the moorland walk ahead.*

Without entering the farmyard turn left along a vague track outside the farm wall. At the next gate a reedy, part-sunken way runs on to emerge onto the open moor. *Look back to appreciate Birk Nab, rising to 1015 feet, and a classic example of a Tabular Hill. Some distance to left and right are its neighbours, Boon Hill and Roppa Edge, respectively.* **Now engulfed in heather, a smashing old way offers real red carpet treatment. Unfortunately it ends too soon, after a sunken descent to the rough road onto Pockley Moor.** *The Hanging Stone named on the OS map is probably the humble rock on the left at this point. The track we join here is the course of a very ancient north-south moorland road, known as 'Thurkilsti'.*

The big track is followed for almost a mile along the broad ridge, rising gently to a crossroads of tracks. Turn left to drop down to Bonfield Gill again. Here, at Cindergill Wath, are the remains of medieval iron workings. Enjoying an easier crossing, climb the slope until just past the wall corner. Here the main track is vacated in favour of a narrower green path, which rises more steadily across the heather on the left to join the open road to Bransdale.

The ruinous kiln at Old Kiln

The walk can be reduced to about five miles, and forestry avoided, by turning left back to the start on the verges of the traffic free road. Otherwise, cross straight over the road and along the farm track opposite. Turn left at an early fork to drop down to the buildings of Old Kiln, passing a severely crumbled kiln just across to the left. Ahead, a great wall of dark green awaits.

On entering its confines turn immediately left to hurdle a fastened gate, then descend the wall-side. At the bottom a thin path descends a bracken bank to cross Bogmire Gill by stepping stones. On the slope opposite a path rises through the plantation to meet a forest road: head straight up the wide track directly ahead, over the brow to a gate out of the trees. Emerge in style with a great sweep of heather-clad Helmsley Moor, and Potter House Farm ahead: this too was the site of an ancient kiln.

Birk Nab from the north

Follow the left-hand fence away to the second gate, then cross the field to Potter House. Without entering its yard turn back to the left on a hard track across this same field to a gate into a bracken pasture. Contour right across it on a stony track to the barns that were once Snaper Farm. Don't go to the barns, but keep straight on the wall-side to a stile in a fence. After it, leave the track and turn right on a faint green way along the wall-side. At the plantation keep straight on, a broader way running through the trees, currently felled on the left side. Soon the track further improves into a super path, which runs on to eventually join a forest road.

Continue left along it to a merging of three such roads at a gate. Turn down through it to a footbridge and ford, then up to join the Bransdale road again. The church is now just a few yards up to the left.

St. Mary Magdalen, East Moors

15

2

KIRKDALE

START Kirkdale   Grid ref. SE 677855

DISTANCE 4½ miles

ORDNANCE SURVEY MAPS
1:50,000
Landranger 100 - Malton & Pickering
1:25,000
Outdoor Leisure 26 - North York Moors (West)

ACCESS Kirkdale lies just off the A170. Though the church is the obvious starting point, its car park is meant for church visitors. There is parking at the head of the short lane to the church, and also on a broad verge up the little hill just across the ford. Scarborough-Helmsley buses run along the main road.

This walk takes the form of a figure-of-eight, thus offering an even shorter stroll if desired.

◻ *Starting from the ford - which is usually dry, thus making the footbridge superfluous - first note the presence of the famous Kirkdale Cave.* This is located just upstream on the east bank, not by the 'beck'side path, but the broader one a few yards to its right (not a right of way, but almost a quagmire caused by bike tracks and hoof prints). Within a minute this reaches the base of a limestone cliff.

The cave is a dark slit located half-way up, and is in fact a series of passages. Many have clearly scrambled up, but the limestone is well polished and could easily cause a slip. Quarrying work in 1821 revealed some outstanding prehistoric remains, including mammoth, tiger, lion and rhinoceros. In view of the narrow height of the entrance, it is thought this would have been a hyenas' den, to which their varied diet was dragged.

The beckside path makes a somewhat overgrown alternative start, tracing it to where the beck bends away, there gaining the main route by a footbridge.

Incidentally, the road here was the main highway until by-passed many decades ago. **Getting going then, cross the ford and up to the short-lived lane to St Gregory's Minster.** *It might be visited now or at the end, but either way, it should be. Unimaginitive entries in the visitors book invariably read 'peaceful', but to be fair, it is the first word that comes to mind: the secluded setting is near perfect. The church dates back to the mid 11th century, replacing an earlier structure torn down by the Danes. A Saxon doorway is now merely an arch into the base of the much more recent tower. The age of the place has been made easy to calculate by virtue of the minster's pride and joy, a Saxon sundial above the entrance door. This remarkable feature's good repair is thanks in great part to the fact it was covered by plaster for several centuries. The translation of its two main panels is thus:*

> Orm the son of Gamel acquired St. Gregory's when it was completely ruined and collapsed, and he had it built anew from the ground to Christ and to St. Gregory, in the days of king Edward and in the days of earl Tostig.

Inside the church, some fine Saxon tomb slabs are just some of the venerable sights. Today much restoration work is needed to save this wonderful place from falling down, and it is hoped all visitors will make their contribution to such a worthy cause.

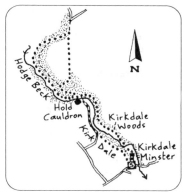

Continuing past the church a track runs into a field, and crosses to a bridge over Hodge Beck. If this is still awaiting repair, there is a footbridge just a little downstream, beyond a ford. *The riverbed is normally completely dry in this lower section of the walk, as - is often the case in limestone country - the Hodge Beck (better known in its upper reaches in Bransdale) takes a subterranean course further upstream. We shall soon see it in more traditional mode.*

The track heads across a pasture to a gate into the woods. *A short way on is a crossroads of tracks. Go straight on up to a waymark at a fork, then bear left on the better path.* This runs in fine style along the foot of the wood, then makes a more sustained pull as a broader way with some open views over the valley. Quickly however it returns to the valley floor to join the broad track of Caldron Mill Road adjacent to the beck. And this time it is the beck, in full flow over a little ledge alongside the old mill. It is just a short way below here that it begins its subterranean passage. For a short version of the walk, omitting a lengthy climb, cross the bridge and follow the road away. Otherwise, **engage the further half of this figure-of-eight by not crossing the bridge**, for now, but heading off along the track.

Saxon sundial, St. Gregory's Minster

Very soon, as it turns to climb away, leave by a stile on the left into a field. A faint green way runs delightfully along this beckside pasture. The old mill cut runs just to our left: the collapsed remnants of a weir might also be seen before the way eventually runs out of field. **A clear track runs on through trees, but quickly returns us to another field. Running tranquilly on outside the wood, keep an eye out for a stile back into it part-way along.** Although the tangle of undergrowth may look daunting, in fact it hides a super path that resumes our journey, never straying far from the foot of the wood. **Under half a mile from entering the wood, and just beyond a branch path from a gate on the left, take the broad pathway slanting up to the right.**

This superb part-hollowed old bridleway ran down to the ford at Cogg Hole Wath and thence to Skiplam Grange. It gives us a sustained but pleasurable pull up through the trees. **A broader track is joined**: a right turn on this track used as a bridleway is the quicker way back. **Turning left, another, shorter, pull soon ensues to rise onto a more solid track. This is the Caldron Mill Road. Turn right to trace a grand, leafy stroll**, free from woodland for a section to enjoy

St. Gregory's Minster, Kirkdale

spacious views, including far ahead beyond the plain to the Wolds.
At the end it re-enters the woods, and winds down to meet the aforementioned 'middle' track. Keep left and it soon returns us to the mill.

This time cross the bridge. *Note the very attractive old mill building and house (Caldron Mill) and also the sadly collapsing buildings on the left.* **Head away along the access road. Passing a 'walkers' car park, this runs on beneath the woods before the anticipated climb commences.** *Part-way up, a well preserved limekiln is passed, just beyond which is a limestone cliff that was clearly once quarried.*

Fine views over Kirkdale are enjoyed before the climb suddenly ends and the road heads away. Here take a gate on the left. *A thin, clear path heads away through a tangle of undergrowth, but within minutes escapes by a gate into a field on the right.* **Resume outside the wood top, along two field's-lengths during which the minster is well seen directly below. A gateway at the end leads down onto the head of the lane to the church.**

Hold Caldron Mill

20

3

BRANSDALE

START Cockayne   Grid ref. SE 620983

DISTANCE   6 ¼ miles

ORDNANCE SURVEY MAPS
1:50,000
Landranger 94 - Whitby
1:25,000
Outdoor Leisure 26 - North York Moors (West)

ACCESS Cockayne stands at the head of Bransdale, 10 miles from Helmsley and Kirkbymoorside. Park on the roadside near the cattle-grid beneath the church.

A straightforward walk on excellent tracks, with far-reaching views over Bransdale and Farndale. No wet feet and little chance of going astray!

Cockayne, though barely a hamlet, is the largest settlement in Bransdale. Along with Bransdale Lodge, still a shooting lodge, is the tiny church of St. Nicholas, an isolated gem. It was erected in 1886 on a much older site, and has an interesting barrelled ceiling. Downstream of Cockayne is a former oatmeal mill which ceased its operations in the 1930's. Much of the upper dale is National Trust property. A glance at the Landranger map reveals Bransdale's 'hidden' location, a great bowl of an upper valley that narrows remarkably at its 'foot', where the Hodge Beck escapes to begin a new life above Kirkdale.

❑ **From the cattle-grid take the Kirkbymoorside road down across the beck. At the first bend up the other side, turn left through a gate and follow a track into the large plantation of Bloworth Wood.** The forest track is not a public right of way, but is open to walkers *courtesy of the Forestry Commission. The well sufaced track exhibits an uncharacteristic lack of the usual claustrophobic conditions.* **After a short pull, the track steadies out for a lengthy spell.** *Much recent felling has opened things out further. As the wood narrows, purple moorland on the outside becomes more evident.*

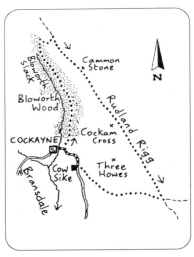

At the top end of the trees the track approaches open moor. Turn right through the gate, and within five minutes the track has us on the top of Rudland Rigg. *Bloworth Crossing is easily identified by the grassy railway embankment a little further north - see WALK 4. The rough road along Rudland Rigg is an ancient highway linking the villages north and south of the high moors. Kirkbymoorside and Ingleby Greenhow tend to dominate the numerous standing stones along its route. Our section gives some glorious views down into both Bransdale and Farndale.*

Turn right along the splendid old road as it favours first the Bransdale and then the Farndale side of the broad ridge. *Three inscribed stones of great interest are encountered during our section of the road. First is the ancient Cammon Stone astride the parish boundary, sporting a Hebrew inscription meaning 'Hallelujah', a curious groove, and a more easily identifiable benchmark. Next is Cockam (Cockayne) Cross, an old guidepost set back from the road. Most prominent of its inscriptions are 'Bransdale Rode' and 'Farndale Rd', though it*

Cammon Stone, Rudland Rigg

also features the main objectives of the rigg road as 'Stoxl (Stokesley) Rode' and 'Kirby (Kirkbymoorside) Rode'. The shorter upper section of the shaft stands tidily in the base, with the lower half recumbent alongside. The third stone is not marked on the OS map, this being another old guidepost inscribed 'Kirby Rode'. In the background are the Bronze age burial cairns of Three Howes.

The old road is our course for well over two miles, until a crossroads with a track of equal stature. Turn right along it, crossing a tiny beck before starting to descend with glorious views over lonely Bransdale. On departing the moor, the track quickly joins the road at Cow Sike. Turn right to return, very shortly, to the start point.

St. Nicholas, Cockayne

4

FARNDALE HEAD

START   Church Houses   Grid ref. 643002

DISTANCE   5¾ miles

ORDNANCE SURVEY MAPS
1:50,000
Landranger 94 - Whitby
1:25,000
Outdoor Leisure 26 - North York Moors (West)

ACCESS   From Church Houses, Farndale, drive along the
'no through road' signposted 'Dale End (East)' for 2½ miles,
and park on the verge after crossing Gill Beck. Apart from
the mileage it is easily found as just up the hill beyond, at Elm
House Farm (the last house up the dale), the surfaced road
ends. There is ample turning space here. Please be sure to
take extra care on this narrow country lane, as there are a
number of farms, and possibly children playing. There is
further parking by the road immediately before the drop to
the bridge.

*Excellent valley and moorland tracks are linked to produce a
surprisingly easy walk through gloriously colourful surroundings.*

*Church Houses is the only gateway to the dale head farms, and
thus to our walk also. A charming place, it has an inn (the
Feversham Arms) 'dedicated' to the local landowner, and also St.
Mary's church, two minutes up the road to Low Mill. Rebuilt in
1871, in the Middle Ages a community of friars existed here.
Hidden in trees, its setting is idyllic. En route to the start, we also
pass the Farndale Dairy Goats Farm at Oak House, which is open
to visitors, with produce available.*

■ *From Gill Beck follow the road uphill to its demise at Elm House Farm, and continue between the buildings on the farm track which takes over. It continues as a level green way before dropping to cross a beck, rising steeply and less clearly up the other side to the ruinous farm of Middle Heads.* This dwelling, clearly once of substance, commands a glorious view down the valley. *Beyond it, avoid a branch up to the right, and remain with the left-hand wall to a gateway.* One has a benchmark, while the other bears seven identical, vertical slots for retaining its old gate. *Go on through bracken, which is soon left behind to wind down to a footbridge across the river Dove.*

The head of Farndale is truly beautiful country: a hint rugged, with lovely trees persisting up the bracken slopes to the Dove's beginnings. As recently as the late 1960's, Hull Corporation were still seeking to build a reservoir here. 'Nuff said.

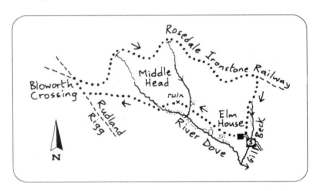

A sketchy path heads along the opposite bank of the river through rather damp terrain to two forlorn gateposts. Continue beyond them to soon rise towards a prominent gate in a wall. From it look across the infant river to see a whole network of fields inside the dale-head intake wall, which have long since been reclaimed by nature following the demise of the dale head farm. *Now a path rises away from the wall, aiming clearly for the head of a side gill. At this point the old railway is very close over to the right. In this slightly confusing quarter, the logical route traces the clearer path across the head of the little gill, from where things ease out, bearing up left to follow a pronounced grassy mound moving from bilberry to heather. This runs on to fade yards before reaching the old railway.*

In fact, one should rise directly up from the head of the gill on a fainter way through the heather, to gain a row of superior grouse butts. Midway along them a landrover track is picked up in deep heather: here the ridge top is gained, and Bloworth Crossing comes into sight with Urra Moor further to the left. When the track swings left before the final butt, go straight on to join the Rudland Rigg road, now just a few yards away. The Rudland Rigg 'road' is an ancient highway explored more fully in WALK 3. **Turn right along this broad track to Bloworth Crossing.** *Just yards before the crossing, an old stone guidepost stands by the track, inscribed with the names Kirkbymoorside and Guisborough.*

Elm House, Farndale

Bloworth Crossing marks the junction of the old road with the one time ironstone railway, and today serves as a junction for long-distance walkers. Here the Coast to Coast Walk parts company with the Cleveland Way. **Turn right along the track bed of the old railway, at once on an embankment.** *Looking back, the Rudland Rigg road stretches away above the head of Bransdale. The old railway line contours around the head of Farndale and, keeping below the watershed, provides spectacular views down the length* of the dale. *It is now followed to the right for two and a half straightforward miles around the headwaters of the river Dove.*

Just beyond a gate preventing unauthorised vehicular use is a small embankment: between these two features we leave the track at a fallen stone (with benchmark) by descending to the highly prominent wooded head of Gill Beck directly below. The railway, meanwhile, continues to Blakey and round the head of Rosedale - see WALK 5.

The waterfall, Gill Beck

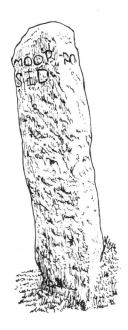

Though pathless, a way can be found which is mostly on grass. On reaching the trees they will be found to hide the beginning of a deep ravine with a fine waterfall pouring over the edge. This is a superb finish down colourful Gill Beck, with bilberry, heather, bracken, rowan trees and the cheerful sound of water.

A good path now materialises to run above the trees on the right side, and descending to depart the moor at a gate. A sunken track drops down through the fields to a briefly enclosed way, which emerges almost immediately onto the road end at Elm House, only yards above the start point.

Guidestone, Rudland Rigg

27

5

ROSEDALE HEAD

START Blakey   Grid ref. SE 683989

DISTANCE 5¼ miles

ORDNANCE SURVEY MAPS
1:50,000
Landranger 94 - Whitby
1:25,000
Outdoor Leisure 26 - North York Moors (West)

ACCESS Start from the moorland car park on the Hutton-le-Hole to Castleton road, at the Farndale junction half a mile south of the *Lion Inn*. Blakey is served by a seasonal Moorsbus service.

An excellent walk around the valley head, from the perfect platform of a former railway line. IMPORTANT: Please note the entire length of the old railway on this walk is not a public right-of-way. It has been a regular walkers' route for many years, courtesy of the landowners. Please respect this fact, and let's keep in the good books by keeping to the line.

The Lion Inn *dates back over 400 years: just behind, on Blakey Howe, is a former cockpit. Once thriving with iron and coal miners, today it refreshes countless walkers and tourists. Ralph Cross stands on the roadside 1¾ miles north of the inn, only a hundred or so feet below the summit of the moors. It marks a meeting of moor roads, and was chosen as the National Park emblem.*

Ralph Cross, Rosedale Head

❏ *From the car park follow the tasteful old footpath sign for Rosedale and immediately the old railway track is met. At the outset, the entire route can now be surveyed. For now go only a yard or two to the right and then head down the slope on a sketchy path. Soon a wide track is met, and this takes us more gently down to Moorlands Farm. Leave by the surfaced access road to drop down to cross the infant river Seven, then rise up to a T-junction. Take the road left to its demise at Dale Head Farm.*

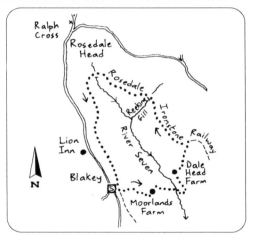

Just level with the house use a gate on the right ('Bridleway to Great Fryup Dale') to pass around the right of a huge hay barn, from where a path rises with a fence above the beck. Higher up it trends right to a gate onto the open moor, and a little further up through the bracken the old railway is encountered again. This time we are to become well acquainted. On first gaining it, turn to see the line running along to the former East Mines: the rows of old ovens can be seen. **The line is now accompanied to the left all the way round the dale head and back to the start point.**

On rounding the first bend, our route ahead appears. Prominent on the skyline is the Lion Inn. A particularly fine moment is the early crossing of a heather-clad embankment at Reeking Gill. In several instances where the line is reed-choked, the path escapes onto an easier, parallel course. A discernible though hardly arduous pull leads to, and past, the remains of a 'winding house', now reduced to one wall. Beyond it, the starting point is quickly reached.

The railside ruin, looking across Rosedale Head

The Rosedale Ironstone Railway was constructed in 1861 to carry vast amounts of iron ore from the Rosedale mines to the furnaces on Tees-side. One cannot fail to be impressed by this achievement of engineering: running across the moors 1000 feet up, the single line climbed from the valley by way of a steep incline then contoured around the head of Farndale to Blakey, where our walk begins.

The car park stands on Blakey Ridge's narrowest point, and a junction developed here in 1865 when the line to the mines on the west side of Rosedale was joined by the line we are returning on, round the dalehead from the East Mines. Here was to be found the only bridge on the whole 20 miles of the railway. The railway closed in 1929 after the demise of the mining industry, but both have left their mark. Today it is difficult to visualise a scene of thousands labouring - and living hard - in this now tranquil dale.

The Lion Inn, Blakey

6

HARLAND MOOR

START   Lowna   Grid ref. SE 685910

DISTANCE   5½ miles

ORDNANCE SURVEY MAPS
1:50,000
Landranger 94 - Whitby **or**
           100 - Malton & Pickering
1:25,000
Outdoor Leisure 26 - North York Moors (West)

ACCESS   Start from the small car park just west of Lowna
Farm on the Gillamoor to Hutton-le-Hole road.

*Lowna is nothing more than a farmstead, but from the road down
to the bridge the prominent large old building was once a tannery.
This is a delightful setting by the river Dove, with the steep
Gillamoor Bank rising to that village, less than a mile distant.*

❑ **From the car park don't return to the road, but instead take the
track leaving the rear of the parking area. It soon narrows to drop
down to cross a beck (footbridge and ford), turning downstream a
few yards to a guidepost and fork. Take the left one which soon
passes beneath an old Quaker burial ground.** *Easily missed, this
takes the form of a small, walled enclosure at the bottom corner
of a wood. A notice by the gate records the fact that between the
years 1675 and 1837, 114 Friends were buried on this site.*

**The path now rises gently alongside a wall across the bottom of
Harland Moor.** *Harland Moor is a fine area of moorland divided by
the Gillamoor-Low Mill road: colourful bracken slopes, interspersed
with rowan, descend almost to the river.* **At a gate into woodland,
take the path down to a junction above the river, and then turn**

upstream. Two ways have been tramped here: one is the broader trackway which keeps well above the beck's immediate environs, the other is a slender path that keeps faith with the wooded bank. The upper one makes an easier walk, gradually narrowing to delve into the silver birch and drop down towards the beck at the end. The lower one forges narrowly but clearly through rampant bracken, before climbing back up to join the main path. Within a minute or so of the meeting, the path arrives at Dale End footbridge on the Dove.

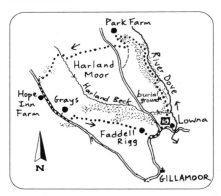

Having broken free of its daffodil following above Low Mill, the river Dove settles down to flow through some exquisitely wooded and very peaceful environs. Shunning any further publicity it glides out of the park to join the river Rye in the Vale of Pickering. While the daffodils extend much further, the public paths don't.

Don't cross the river but take the path climbing steeply left: it soon eases to swing right, with the bracken-clad moor over the fence on the left. Ignore a stile in it (or take it and forge up through virgin bracken) and keep straight on this level course. When the way swings left towards a blocked fence, advance straight on a slender path through trees. Quickly reaching a gate, a broad green track then climbs up to the left. Through a gate it slants up under a scattering of trees. At the top it meets a drive to isolated Park Farm. Turn left along it to quickly gain the open country of Harland Moor.

Advance along this drive for a further 130 or so yards, then locate a slender path doubling back up to the right (50 yards short of a stile in a fence down to the left). Once found it is completely clear as it slants up the moor, with glorious views into the heart of Farndale. It quickly runs above a wall-corner and onto a moorland road.

At a pair of footpath signs cross straight over and along a good landrover track through the heather of Harland Moor. Above the road Harland Moor is a classic heather terrain, with views now to the south of a range of Tabular Hills. Boon Hill, and to its right Birk

Boon Hill from Harland Moor

Nab, are prominent. **Decending gradually it eventually leaves the moor at a gate, and a short way along the wall-side a gate on the left precedes a footbridge over Harland Beck.** *The adjacent ford is worth using in order not to miss a remarkable spring just a couple of yards upstream. At our feet is the answer to the red beck, for the chalybeate spring, within a yard of the stream on the bank, spills forth a gaudy hue of iron-coloured water into the previously clear stream, quite impressive!*

Take the path doubling back up to the wall, then rising by a crumbling wall to a wall corner, crossing a rough pasture to a gate between wall and fence. From it take the slender but clear path through the heather, slanting diagonally crossing across a curious little moor interspersed with conifers to a gate onto a road.

Turn left along the road past Hope Inn Farm, to soon drop down to pass Grays Farm set back on the left. *This farmstead has the appearance of the Danish-style long house.* **Continue two fields further to the start of a steep climb, and then escape left at a bridleway sign and a gate. Drop down to another gate and then sharp right on an enclosed way. Initially rather overgrown, this improves beyond the next gate to quickly become a cart-track. Just beyond a wooded area is a fork, the right arm leaving the trees to run between hedgerows to Faddell Rigg Farm, continuing past it onto the road.**

Turn left along the road to soon return to the car park just beyond the Farndale junction.

Lowna Farm

33

FARNDALE

START Low Mill   Grid ref. SE 672952

DISTANCE 6¾ miles

ORDNANCE SURVEY MAPS
1:50,000
Landranger 94 - Whitby *or*
            100 - Malton & Pickering
1:25,000
Outdoor Leisure 26 - North York Moors (West)

ACCESS Start from the village centre. There is a small car park, very quickly filled on a good day.

Farndale is rightly renowned for its springtime carpet of daffodils, the result being a one-way road system and little chance to wander lonely as a cloud. Don't be put off by this - any crowds will soon be left behind. The reason for this profusion of yellow has been attributed to the monks of Rievaulx and also to Nicholas Postgate, 'martyr of the moors', who dubbed them 'lenten lilies'. Whatever their beginnings, it was their threatened disappearance that prompted designation of the Farndale Nature Reserve in 1953, and woe betide any souvenir hunters today.

❑ *From the car park first appraise the idyllic picture postcard scene presented by the Post office across the road, then take the adjacent gate to a footbridge over the river. The path now follows the Dove upstream, and as this forms the 'daffodil walk' (in season) there is little chance of going astray.* Note how the meandering Dove covers twice the ground we do! *Numerous stiles are encountered on this path - that is ever being 'improved' - before arrival at High Mill, a narrow lane now taking us away from the river to Church Houses.*

While at Church Houses a worthwhile visit (besides the Feversham Arms) *is to St. Mary's church, two minutes up the road to Low Mill. Rebuilt in 1871, in the Middle Ages a community of friars existed here. Hidden in trees, its setting is idyllic.*

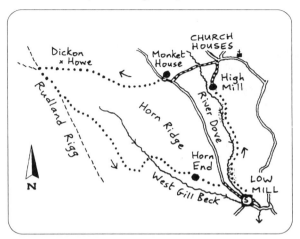

At the first road junction turn left to re-cross the Dove before a steep climb to another junction. *Here we have earned a grand view across the dale, with Blakey Ridge on the skyline and the steep Blakey Bank descending to Church Houses and the patchwork fields of the valley. To the left the tree-lined river leads the eye to the inviting dalehead, scene of WALK 4.* **Here turn right only as far as Monket House, then take the second gate on the left, opposite the rear buildings. A rutted track climbs the rough pasture to a gate onto the moor, passing old quarries before easing out to stride through luxuriant heather.** *At the dalehead is a skyline formed by the Rosedale ironstone railway, while looking back, the Bilsdale TV mast appears over Rudland Rigg.* **A prominent cairn on Dickon Howe is observed before reaching a crossroads with the Rudland Rigg 'road'.**

The old road along Rudland Rigg is a splendid walkers' highway, and was once a major route between the communities north and south of the moorland barrier. Whilst on it our views are largely confined to the parallel ridges of Bilsdale Moors to the right and Blakey Ridge to the left. Ahead is a whole array of Tabular Hills.

*The cairn on
Dickon Howe*

Here turn left for a little under half a mile, and just encountering a gentle rise, turn off left on a heathery shooters' track. This is accompanied steadily down past a string of grouse butts. Towards the end of these, a narrower path takes up a generally level course through bracken and heather. Between West Gill and the main valley, the clean-cut profile of Horn Ridge dominates the secluded, richly coloured side-valley. Where are those daffodil throngs now?

Keep straight on at a tiny stream, and remain on a level path contouring on to the edge of a pronounced drop, now marked by

*High Mill,
Farndale*

a cairn. Don't descend the obvious way with a wall corner just down to the left, but bear right along the level brow. The head of a dry gill is quickly reached. Take the left branch which contours round before winding down a short way. It then runs on through bracken, very clearly beneath the roughness of Double Crag.

From a minor reedy tract at the end, drop down to a gate in the wall just below. From it a green path swings down to the left, doubling back on a track that forms. This leaves the field at a stile in the wall on the left, from where drop down to a footbridge over West Gill Beck. Turn right to shortly rise to a barn, from where a level track heads away to Horn End Farm. Continue away on its access track to drop down to a road, with Low Mill now only five minutes along to the right.

Looking down to Farndale from the head of West Gill

8

GILLAMOOR

START Hutton-le-Hole   Grid ref. SE 704901

DISTANCE 6¾ miles

ORDNANCE SURVEY MAPS
1:50,000
Landranger 94 - Whitby *or*
          100 - Malton & Pickering
1:25,000
Outdoor Leisure 26 - North York Moors (West)

ACCESS Start from the village centre. Large car park at the top end, on the moor-edge. Also served by seasonal Moorsbus, but otherwise a very occasional service.

Hutton-le-Hole is probably the best-known inland village in the National Park, and in summer its popularity is all too evident. Its charms are open to view, with the beck, its bridges and its ubiquitous sheep tending its extensive 'green'. The Crown inn and some tearooms offer refreshment. Things to look for include the old cattle pound and tiny St. Chad's church with the mouseman's work. Hutton's position is also superb, sheltering under the Tabular Hills with moors rising to the north. Aside from its obvious charms, Hutton's special feature is Ryedale Folk Museum. Its excellent presentation of local life in bygone days is crowned by a range of reconstructed moor dwellings. It is open late March to late October, and has numerous special event days.

❑ *From the village centre take the Castleton road, and leave it by a stile on the left where the parallel side road comes in (after the last house on the left). Go right with the hedge to a corner stile, bear left to a gate opposite, then on again to a stile. A few yards further, turn right onto a hedgerowed way. Turn left along this grand, leafy way to its demise, then continue along a cornfield side to emerge onto a bracken-cloaked heath.*

Ahead is a grand expanse of moorland, Harland Moor and beyond, and a range of Tabular Hills to the left. **Choose the green path bearing left, but at an early fork take the better one bearing right across the heather of the common. Within fifty yards, however, take a slimmer, grassy path right, quickly escaping bracken to descend slowly, making for red roofed Grouse Hall ahead.**

Savour this open section with its free roaming and open views. Somewhere on the wooded bank opposite is Gillamoor, camouflaged in foliage. **Entering bracken again, our superior green way crosses a drain, then another such way merges as we descend to a fence corner. Down its side, a farm track is quickly joined. Go right a few yards then drop to a footbridge and into a field. Cross straight over to a stile and across again to one in the next field corner.** *A fence is then followed down to a wooden footbridge on the Dove.*

From the bridge advance to a rustic barn, and on to a gate leading round the back of the old mill. Its access track is accompanied uphill until above a sharp bend. With climbing virtually complete, double back on a path that contours along to the left before swinging up beneath a steep, wooded bank. This excellent, part-hollowed way rises up to emerge into Gillamoor.

Gillamoor is a street village on the edge of a plateau, and is renowned for its surprise view: Farndale, Lowna and Blakey Ridge feature in a glorious vista from just north of St. Aidan's church. Dating from 1802 and restored in 1880, its absence of windows to north and east is a sign of respect for the elements: it also boasts a Norman font. Note also the freestanding stone sundial in the main street, and a tearoom further along the street. **A tablet at Surprise View reads:**

'Though who hast given me eyes to see
And love this sight so fair
Give me a heart to find out thee
And read thee everywhere'
J.Keble.

Head along the street and left at the junction by the **Royal Oak** *and the* **Post office**, *then leave the road at the first bend by taking the narrow lane straight ahead. At an early kink in it take a stile on the left and follow the fence away alongside the cricket field. Stiles lead through a couple more fields before crossing to the far corner across the last one before the trees. Just beyond is a gate, and a track down through a wood.*

After a brief spell of freedom from the trees, the wood is re-entered only for the same thing to happen further on. A long sketchy section between river and forest in Douthwaite Dale now ensues. Douthwaite Dale is the southern continuation of Farndale, and relates to the short length of the valley where the Dove breaks through the Tabular Hills to leave the moor.

A little further, the trees are entered yet again. At a crossroads just ahead, the easiest way is the broad track climbing steeply ahead. At the top it merges into another track and heads away along the

Gillamoor Mill

forest top. Correctly, the bridleway bears along the broad track to the left. It is left just beyond the end of the plantation on the left, where a thinner way slants up. This rises to a level green track at mid-height. Go left a few yards, then turn up a broad track to reach a hairpin bend - go right to join the top forest road, and turn left.

In time a surfaced road with useful verges takes over. Part-way along the surfaced section, immediately beyond a timber yard, a footpath sign sends a tightly enclosed way down into trees. This soon opens out and descends to join the road below Ravenswick.

Turn left to the road-end at the riverbank. Take the left track to a footbridge over the Dove, noting the old mill and its former cut. Follow a rough trackway climbing away to the open country of Hutton Common. On easing to meet the Douthwaite Dale farm road, extensive views open out over the dale, to Harland Moor and beyond. Just short of the Kirkbymoorside to Hutton-le-Hole road, a short-cut across the common cuts out a tiny bit of road walking. On the brow cross over the main road. For a straightforward finish turn left, with its large proportion of grass verges, to drop down into the village.

A more interesting conclusion leaves the road at a gate set back on the right, just as the road is about to commence its descent towards the red roofs of Hutton. A path heads away through undergrowth, turning left into a wood to drop to a footbridge on Hutton Beck. A steep little pull past the plantation opposite leads, by bearing left above the trees, to a gate onto a wide track. Turn left along this drive to soon arrive back in the village.

Hutton-le-Hole

41

9

APPLETON-LE-MOORS

START Sinnington   Grid ref. SE 744857

DISTANCE 5 miles

ORDNANCE SURVEY MAPS
1:50,000
Landranger 94 - Whitby *or*
              100 - Malton & Pickering
1:25,000
Outdoor Leisure 26 - North York Moors (West)
                27 - North York Moors (East)

ACCESS Start from the bridge in the village centre. There is ample parking alongside the broad greens, without encroaching on them. Sinnington is served by Scarborough-Helmsley buses.

Sinnington is a peaceful village, happily by-passed by the main road. Though restored in 1904, All Saints' church boasts some Norman and Saxon work, and fragments of Anglo-Saxon and Danish crosses. A barn opposite was originally part of a 12th century hall: its east window dates from then, the others three centuries later.

For two and a half centuries the village has been home to the Sinnington hunt, and a fox graces the maypole. The pub is another reminder of this country pastime. Note the defunct little pack-bridge near the graceful central bridge of 1767.

☐ ***Leave the village by the road heading up the east side of the river above the bridge by the green. Passing a fork to the church, the road becomes a track at the last house and drops down to the river.*** *To the right is a most impressive high limestone scar.* ***When the Seven loops away the track continues along the bottom of the***

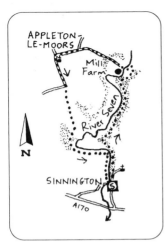

wood, soon rising a little to a crossroads in the trees on a tiny ridge. Here turn up to the right but very soon leave the track on a bend and continue straight up on a narrow path.

Levelling out, the path leaves Spring Bank Wood at a stile. Here turn down to the corner of the wood, then head away above a tree-lined bank to a stile into Hob Bank Wood. An excellent path now runs above the river before dropping down to its bank.

When the Seven loops away again we continue once more along the bottom of the wood. **At a fork take the rising path to another crossroads on a small ridge, and cross straight over to a track descending the other side. The wood is left along a short enclosed way, at the end of which resist the slope in front but turn left to the riverbank. Just downstream is a modern footbridge over the Seven.**

The footbridge has replaced the far more interesting ford at the weir at Appleton Mill Farm just a little further downstream. Other than in times of spate, the concrete weir provided a safe river crossing and a boot cleaning service. Ducks abound in this setting, and the old mill and its cut still survive: unfortunately this characterful corner is now just off our route.

*Low Cross,
Appleton*

43

Turn downstream from the bridge, and the farm access road is met. This immediately climbs away, enjoying the walk's first open views over to the right, with Hutton Ridge and Cropton Forest visible. Joining a narrow lane, continue straight up, with the tall spire of Appleton church appearing on the brow. A T-junction is soon reached at the top of Appleton-le-Moors village. Note, on the verge on the right, Appleton Low Cross, an ancient waymarker. *Turn left to take in the entire length of the main street.*

Appleton-le-Moors

Appleton-le-Moors is a classically laid out village with a broad main street, our traverse of which is likely to induce the theme tune of High Noon. Parallel back lanes run along the rear of both rows of gradely dwellings. The distinguished Christ Church dates from 1865, and a Wesleyan chapel from 1832. The Moors Inn offers refreshment, and keep your eyes peeled for the house of three faces.

At the sharp bend at the far end keep straight on down a short farm track, emerging into a field. Wide views are now on offer, over the Seven woodlands of our walk to the Wolds beyond the Vale of Pickering. Descending on a good track, Sinnington itself appears ahead. *The track upgrades to a path down the hedge-side, very much a wildlife corridor. At a gate causing a tiny kink in the accompanying hedge, pass through and cross to a gate into Bishop Hagg Wood. Before entering, pause to look back upon a glorious wooded surround, a scene which could be many miles from civilisation.*

A good path resumes high above the river to a gate back out of the trees. From here a wide track clings to the tree-lined Seven. Though it is the river of Rosedale, the Seven's finest moments are here above Sinnington, where it loops through some exquisite and popular wooded environs. The track leads unerringly back into Sinnington, with the bridge returning us to the main part of the village.

The bridge at Sinnington

10

ROSEDALE

START Rosedale Abbey   Grid ref. SE 724959

DISTANCE 5½ miles

ORDNANCE SURVEY MAPS
1:50,000
Landranger 94 - Whitby **or**
          100 - Malton & Pickering
1:25,000
Outdoor Leisure 26 - North York Moors (West)

ACCESS Start from the village centre - there are two car parks nearby. There is a rare bus service from Pickering.

Rosedale Abbey is a lovely village in the true heart of the National Park. It is also a busy little place, with hostelries, cafes, shops, bakery, Post office and caravan sites. Its name stems from the existance of a Cistercian nunnery founded here in the mid 12th century. What little remains stands forlornly in a small enclosure behind the church (St. Margaret & St. Lawrence, 1839), and is seen at the end of the walk. Much of the stone was plundered for dwellings during the 19th century iron boom (see also WALK 5). Roads radiate from strategically sited Rosedale Abbey, including two which cross the high moors to a wide range of Eskdale villages.

◻ **Leave the village centre at a footpath sign midway between the car park opposite the green, and the toilets just a little further along the road to Castleton. A short enclosed way soon empties into a field, and here we turn left to head upstream with Northdale Beck. The barely discernible path keeps company with the beck through numerous fields.** *The tributary of Northdale Beck flows through a little-known valley, its banks remaining wooded almost all the way to its source.*

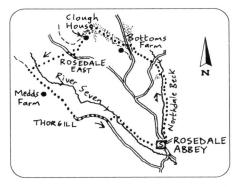

When the right of way finally slants up to a gate, remain on the beckside path, as new ladder-stiles convey a concessionary path all the way to a wooden footbridge that has replaced a tiny slab bridge. The higher level path crosses a field to a smaller gate before returning to the beck, and the bridge.

From the bridge take the green way heading right alongside a wall, continuing on above the trees to join a steep farm road. Cross straight over and a green path slants across the field, enjoying splendid views over upper Northdale. Pass through a gate and on to the top corner of a fence at the start of a tiny beck. Walk by the fence to join a green track rising from a ruin by an old reservoir on the right. This climbs to a plantation: don't enter, but take the track doubling back up to the left, soon leaving this for a direct one onto the adjacent road. The original footpath has been diverted here, so go right a few yards to a stile. Enjoy now the rare prospect of two valleys at this point, with Rosedale to the left and Northdale to the right. This briefly narrow section of the ridge is shared with the road, and is also the highest point of the walk.

Rosedale Abbey:
church and
nunnery ruins

Waterhouse Well,
Rosedale Abbey

From the stile a path heads on through the mixed plantation. This is the terminal section of the old ironstone railway line. Keep straight on, through a denser plantation, which opens out a little just before the sharp bend at a stream crossing. Just beyond, locate the departure of the main path down to the left, unconvincingly at first into dense plantation, but then running along to the right to drop to the paddock at Clough House. Here we are diverted again, on a thin path following the fence right, along the foot of the trees to pass along the rear of the buildings to a hurdle stile onto its drive. Follow this right as it heads away to join a better track. Here we gain a fair prospect of the true upper reaches of the dale. Turn down this firmer drive to meet the road in Rosedale East.

Turn right along the road, passing a Primitive Methodist chapel of 1872, now shared with a school field centre. The little community at Rosedale East is a suprising place to find this far up the valley. Here are terraces of former miners' dwellings and, until recently, a most absorbing Post office, one of the last of its breed. Now Moordale House, the only obvious clue to its past life being the Victorian post box still embedded in its wall. In sight from its doorstep is the Lion Inn on Blakey Ridge, along with a good deal of the dalehead.

A footpath sign points down the surfaced road alongside Moordale House. Pass the holiday cottages at Craven Garth, and down into the farmyard. At the bottom continue straight down the field-side, pausing to look back up-dale to see the rows of ovens at the former Rosedale East mine workings: for more on Rosedale's mining (and railway) days, see WALK 5. **At the bottom a footbridge crosses the river Seven. Rise up the field behind to a gate onto a track between hedgerows, and turn left along it.** *A notable length of this road is shadowed by an old flagged causey, grassed over in parts.* **Eventually we meet the road-end at Thorgill.**

Head through the hamlet and remain on the road for a short half-mile until a stile and footpath sign point a super flagged path the way down a field to a footbridge to re-cross the Seven. Turn right along a path which leaves the trees at a stile to soon rise to a fence corner, then running along the fence-top to another stile. A caravan site appears below, and our path eventually merges with its access track at a wicket-gate.

The dog kennel structure alongside the drive here is Waterhouse Well, which once provided water for the priory. The intriguing little shelter built around it is complete with an internal stone seat. **Head along the track passing a recreation area. Here, go left on a short green way to a wall-stile onto a road, emerging by a nice little pond, and just opposite the nunnery remains at the back of the church. Turn right along the back road to locate the green.**

Thorgill

49

11

ANA CROSS

START   Lastingham   Grid ref. SE 729904

DISTANCE   8 miles

ORDNANCE SURVEY MAPS
1:50,000
Landranger 94 - Whitby **or**
            100 - Malton & Pickering
1:25,000
Outdoor Leisure 26 - North York Moors (West)

ACCESS   Start from the village centre, where there is room
for thoughtful parking. An alternative start is the large car
park at Hutton-le-Hole, just off-route, or at many places on
the open road between the two villages. A very occasional
bus service links the villages.

*A first class moorland ramble over two broad ridges. This should
clear the lungs.*

*Lastingham is a delightful village sharing an identical situation to
its near-neighbour Hutton-le-Hole: it shelters beneath wooded*

*Tabular Hills while looking north to
the moors. Here, however, the
similarity soon ends. Firstly,
Lastingham's houses do not stand
quietly back, but huddle round a
compact centre with lanes branching off in all directions. The second
and more notable difference is
that instead of prettiness,
Lastingham's pilgrim comes seeking a shrine, that of St. Cedd.*

Ana Cross

Cedd was a Lindisfarne monk who came and founded a monastery in 654, a task completed by his brother Chad. Destroyed by the Danes two centuries later, the site of this important early Christian centre became a place of pilgrimage. In 1078 Stephen of Whitby built a crypt, and still intact beneath the present church, it is a unique Norman relic, and can be inspected. Also amongst the treasures is an early Anglo-Saxon cross head. Several wells, including one to Cedd, can be found about the village. The Blacksmiths Arms now doubles as the village Post office, a rare but by no means unique feature in northern villages.

☐ **Leave the village centre by the Hutton-le-Hole road between the church and the inn. With its good proportion of grass verges this undulating road is accompanied for 1½ miles, passing en route the attractive cottage groupings at High Cross. Little short of a junction with the moor road from Rosedale Abbey, turn right up a green track through the bracken, crossing straight over the incoming road and up a private road 'to Spaunton Lodge only'. As the track rises above the moor road, far-reaching views of the Tabular Hills open up to the west. Sharp eyes will be able to pick out Ana Cross high on the skyline ahead and to the right.**

This gently rising access track is followed for almost a mile until where it bears left and descends a little, take a green path continuing our more direct journey up the broad ridge. The path improves in quality as it maintains the steady rise, passing through a line of grouse butts to arrive at a T-junction. Here turn right on a shooters' track which is accompanied as far as a sheepfold at the second of two becks encountered. Now leave the track and cross the beck by the fold. Go up a little to skirt a marsh, then slant along to the left. A slim trod forms, then turns to rise pleasantly as a grassy track through the heather onto the moor road.

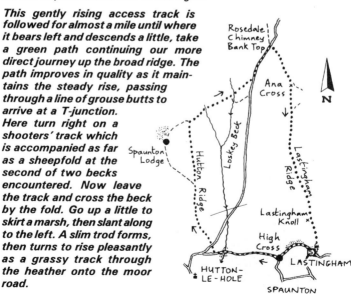

51

On gaining the road turn left up it to the brow of the hill, with another excellent verge to assist. Here we are on Bank Top, overlooking the infamous gradients of Rosedale Chimney Bank as it descends to Rosedale Abbey. This popular motorists' halt is a grand viewpoint, enhanced by advancing nearer the edge from where the rows of old kilns from the ironstone mines can be seen: this was the terminus of the ironstone railway (see WALK 5). The chimney in question stood at the Bank Top, but this tall 19th century mining relic was demolished in 1972.

At this point the ensuing mile is not dedicated as a right of way, though it has been in common use for decades. *Turning right on this wide moortop path, Ana Cross beckons unfailingly on the skyline. A narrower path leaves the main one to gain the cross.* Ana Cross is a striking feature on a prominent rise. The 10ft high cross is a replacement for the original ancient one. This is a truly extensive viewpoint, though the broad uplift of moorland rules out intimate valley scenery. North of the moor road the Three Howes are conspicuous, while to the west and north-east are the rolling moors above Hutton and Rosedale respectively. Southwards are regimented Tabular Hills, and south-east regimented Cropton Forest.

From the cross a clear, cairned path continues due south, merging into a wide track to maintain the long and very gradual return to Lastingham. On Lastingham Knoll the environs of the village finally appear. A nice pairing is formed by the last sighting of Ana Cross, high on the moor, and the appearance of the church embowered in trees below. *A seat suggests one last halt before the track becomes enclosed. Here our walk meets its first and only obstacle, the gate off the moor. A lane descends into the centre of the village, passing an offer of afternoon tea at the Lastingham Grange Hotel.*

Lastingham

12

CAWTHORN CAMPS

START   Newton-on-Rawcliffe   Grid ref. SE 812905

DISTANCE   8 miles

ORDNANCE SURVEY MAPS
1:50,000
Landranger 94 - Whitby *or*
            100 - Malton & Pickering
1:25,000
Outdoor Leisure 27 - North York Moors (East)

ACCESS   Start from the village centre, parking tidily alongside, rather than on, the spacious greens. The only bus from Pickering is classed as a rare sighting. Levisham station on the North Yorkshire Moors Railway is only half a mile distant by footpath. An alternative start is Cawthorn Camps car park (Grid ref. 782895), reached from Cropton or the A170 at Wrelton or Pickering.

Note before starting: if intent on a serious and detailed study of the camps, one might wish to obtain a leaflet in advance from a National Park Centre, as the dispenser at the site is unlikely to be dispensing, thanks to the efforts of vandals, even here.

By a coincidence unknown at the time of researching the walk, the main part of the trek, to just short of Cawthorn Camps, traces a particularly circuitous section of the newly waymarked Link Walk, which meanders along the Tabular Hills fringing the southern area of the National Park. As hinted by its name, it branches off the Cleveland Way in order to form a link with its starting point at Helmsley. A booklet has been produced by the National Park, and is available locally.

Newton is one of a number of villages on the southern fringe of the moors, perched on a breezy plateau of the Tabular Hills overlooking a steep northerly - and here easterly - drop. Its contrasting surrounds find the wooded gorge of Newton Dale on one side, and vast, rolling cropfields on the other. Its layout is also like its Tabular Hills neighbours, being a simple street village with no depth. Though a quiet little place, it is colourful enough, with a duckpond at the centre, looking across to the White Swan pub and a Post office, store and teashop. Its Sunday title of Newton upon Rawcliffe is displayed on the roadsign at the entrance to the village.

❑ *Leave by the road climbing out of the top end of the village, but by the last house turn at a seat on the right. Two ways head off: ignore the one to the right, and take the broad track bearing away from the road, quickly descending the deep woodland of Newton Banks and past a barn.* There are early glimpses to the great heathery tracts of Levisham Moor across Newton Dale. *This hollowed way works down through the trees, then swings left to run along to a small ford at Raygate Slack. Up the other side the track swings along to the right, but our path climbs directly up through the dwindling trees onto the foot of Stony Moor.*

With better views now across to Levisham Moor, the path remains clear throughout a long gentle rise across the well named moor, striding through the rough heather, grass and intermittent trees. While seemingly forging deeper into the middle of nowhere, eventual arrival at the far side comes as quite a shock. Here is a

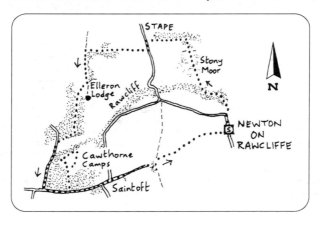

*broad trackway along the moor edge, and a house just ahead.
Cross straight over the track to a gate alongside the house, where
an inviting green track heads away between new plantings. At the
end is a crossroads of pathways. Turn left, along the field-side
above an established plantation above Rain Dale. Forge on through
several fields, transferring by a corrugated barn at the end onto a
firm track climbing out of Rain Dale. This leads straight on to meet
the Stape road opposite Taylor Hill Farm.*

At Cawthorn Camps

**Turn left down the broad verge, and at the first opportunity take
the track along to the right.** *This enclosed way known as the Peat
Road runs straight as an arrow, improving in surface as it passes
an attractive plantation.* **When it turns right at the junction at the
end, take the track left.** *This descends pleasantly along the edge
of the wood to reach the entrance to a driveway. Advance just a
couple of yards onto it, then turn sharp right on the branch drive
to High Cawthorn, across to the right. Leave this at once also,
however, passing through a bridle-gate and on a slender trod
bearing across the field to a gate into woodland opposite.*

The map suggests this is a tract of moorland, when in fact it is quite densely wooded. *A clear path runs away, soon beginning a long, very gradual descent through a rich variety of trees. In time it reaches a footbridge at the bottom, then climbs away to run through the trees out to the Keldy Castle forest road. Turn left, soon climbing the brow before running along to meet the Cropton-Newton road. Turn left to quickly reach the drive to Cawthorn Camps.*

First port of call is a detailed information board in the car park. Those with only a human memory will now appreciate why a leaflet is of value. The trail covers about a mile in distance, and one could easily spend an hour ambling round. Excavated in the 1920's, the site is described as being of unparalleled archaeological importance. This is because it was not a normal fort, but a training, or practice camp. The troops came here not only to practice manouevres intended to maintain their firm grip on their conquered land, but also to practice erecting camps: this explains the different layouts from different periods.

The site was purchased by the National Park Authority in 1983, and required a great deal of work in cutting back the encroaching scrub of many years' neglect, and creating a path network for visitors to appreciate the remains and their setting. The trail is a memorial to Richard Bell MBE, the National Park's first warden, and head ranger from 1974 until his death in 1987. A series of fingerposts serve to confirm the designated clockwise route: as a new leaflet is being prepared, the layout of the route may well change at some point. Visitors are requested to keep to the path, and off the easily eroded banks. The path is not a public right of way.

A path heads away from the northern end of the car park into the trees, quickly reaching the commencement of the trail proper. In front are the very pronounced mounds that indicate the outlines of the former camps. A close look at the layout reveals a central earthwork with two ditches, each with its own pair of trenches. *The path goes part-way round the first camp, then cuts across the centre of it.*

The path leads along the northern edge of an unusual coffin shaped camp, then winds round to the corner of a rectangular camp. Here it turns southwards down its outside before continuing on to return to the starting path.

For the final stage of the walk, follow the drive back out onto the road, and turn left. Keep straight on, past junctions to right (Pickering) and left (Newton), and forge on along Bradley Road. This 'no through road' gradually becomes a track descending into woodland. Risng up the other side, another track, West Dike Road, is met. Turn briefly left along it, until 50 yards past the end of the undergrowth on the left. Here take a gate on the right, and follow the hedge away past grassed over old quarries over to the right.

When the hedge parts company the way is straight ahead, but a better option is to follow the track going left a short way before it turns right to resume the original direction. Things are not as per map here! Ahead, the houses of Newton-on-Rawcliffe are ranged on the skyline. The track makes a long descent of a vast crop field, becoming firmer and eventually arriving at a gate in the bottom corner. Go right a few yards on the broader track there, then turn left to rise between hedgerows back into the centre of Newton village.

Newton-on-Rawcliffe

13

NEWTON DALE

START   Newtondale Halt   Grid ref. 835948

FINISH   Levisham Station   Grid ref. 818910

DISTANCE   4 miles

ORDNANCE SURVEY MAPS
1:50,000
Landranger 94 - Whitby *or*
          100 - Malton & Pickering
1:25,000
Outdoor Leisure 27 - North York Moors (East)

ACCESS This walk makes use of the North Yorkshire Moors Railway to enjoy a linear route. Either Levisham station, or better still Pickering, would make the best start point, then getting the train to Newtondale Halt. Of course one could also catch the train from either Goathland or Grosmont at the northern end. There is also room to park in the vicinity of Levisham station, but far better to leave the car in Pickering.

☐ *Take the access path down from the station, and then take the underpass beneath the line. Ignore the stepping stones, and turn left upstream, between the infant Pickering Beck and the railway in lovely woodland. Crossing a fence, keep on to soon reach a footbridge. Here re-cross and use the footbridge from where a path rises away up the edge of a plantation. There are glimpses of Huggitt's Scar high above, which we shall soon be atop. A stile takes us outside, then climbs more steeply to a welcome seat.*

A wooden staircase avoids a path landslip, to gain a magnificent vantage point at the southern edge of Yewtree Scar as it runs away in great uniformity. Just above is the end of the climb, marked by

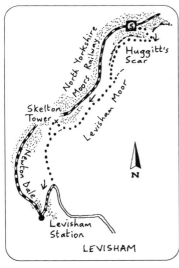

LEVISHAM

a small cairn as we gain the edge at Hudson's Cross. Looking back north, RAF Fylingdales is visible, though the dismantling of the golf balls has left this famous landmark very much emasculated.

Just across the plateau of Levisham Bottoms a further bank rises, but this is the top of the climb for us. **Turn right to begin a classic promenade, with a heather sea to the left and a stupendous drop into Newton Dale on the right.** First thing to do, after rounding the small inlet, is to look back for a second, very different prospect of Yewtree Scar. Despite its cloak of afforestation, Newton Dale remains a dramatic setting by virtue of the deep groove it has carved through the moors. At its northern limit the valley merges tamely with that of Eller Beck, which flows north through Goathland and into Eskdale. This natural pass is the most obvious in the entire breadth of the moors, and was consequently exploited by George Stephenson who constructed his Whitby-Pickering railway through here. The line between Grosmont and Pickering was saved by a preservation society and is now one of the National Park's major attractions.

Skelton
Tower

From here on, it's simply a case of walking along the edge, remembering that young children should be kept on a very tight rein. For some time only a modest trod, the path never strays far from the edge until a swing left sees it join a broad track coming in from the left. This itself now stays quite close to the edge, with the landmark of Skelton Tower increasing in prominence further along the edge. The track eventually arrives at some very interesting old quarries immediately above the drop. As they end, leave the track's direct course and follow the thinner edge path to the tower.

Skelton Tower is a notable landmark, built as a shooting lodge in the early 19th century by the vicar of Levisham, Robert Skelton. A partial restoration by the National Park Authority in 1978 made the ruin safe. This is a fine place to linger, and a favourite vantage point for the steam trains. From here one might simply remain on the edge, though a wall and trees come in to rob the views. If followed it will, however, lead all the way to the road just above the station.

On leaving, take the path directly away from the edge, and at a crossroads turn right along the continuation of our earlier track. (To take in lunch at Levisham - see WALK 15 - keep straight on at the crossroads, up the slanting path up the bank and along the moor to a wall corner. Go left with the wall till it cuts in to a corner, where an enclosed track, Braygate Lane, makes a bee-line for the village.) *This strikes a direct course over this lower level of Levisham Moor, along to meet the road to Levisham Station. Turn down it to finish, with moorland offering an alternative to tarmac almost to the end.*

Yewtree Scar
from
Huggitt's Scar

14

HOLE OF HORCUM

START Saltergate   Grid ref. SE 852937

DISTANCE 7 ½ miles

ORDNANCE SURVEY MAPS
1:50,000
Landranger 94 - Whitby *or*
　　　　　　100 - Malton & Pickering
1:25,000
Outdoor Leisure 27 - North York Moors (East)

ACCESS Start from the large car park above Saltergate Bank on the A169, half a mile south of the inn. Pickering-Whitby buses run along this road.

Very easy walking in truly spectacular surroundings.

◻ **From the car park cross the main road to a path parallel with it, and head north as far as the hairpin bend on Saltergate Bank. Here advance to take a stile down to the left to descend immediately into the Hole of Horcum.** *The Hole of Horcum is a famous feature alongside the busy A169. It takes the form of an enormous bowl which nature has carved out of the moors, and to date it remains untamed by the plough.* **The path heads through bracken to a stile, and continues on past the old farm of Low Horcum. Just beyond, fork right on a narrow trod through a long pasture in the narrowing dale.**

On approaching the wood above, fork right to stay outside its fence, soon crossing a couple of stiles to drop down very gradually to a footbridge over tree-lined Levisham Beck. Crossing this and the inflowing beck just beyond, a guidepost is reached indicating a path up to the right. Turn right to follow a green path up the side of Dundale Griff, a mini-dale that is more than likely to be dry. As height is gained, heather takes over from bracken, while sturdy oaks line the edge of the little ravine. A griff, incidentally, is a very localised word for a small side-valley.

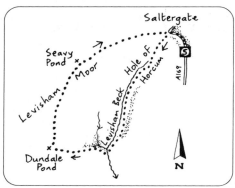

At the moor top take the narrower right fork which runs gently along to Dundale Pond. *The pond is an artificial sheet of water, thought to have been the work of the monks of Malton Priory in the 13th century, to cater for their flocks and herds which grazed here. This reed-fringed pool stands at a busy junction of moorland tracks, and regularly hosts assorted rucksack picnics: it is also a favourite habitat of dragonflies.*

At Dundale Pond

62

From this Piccadilly Circus of tracks turn sharp right on the broadest departing way. This track mounts the brow above the pond, and heads away over the great rolling Levisham Moor. The Levisham estate, incidentally, is owned by the National Park Authority, and visitors are welcome to walk here. *This same track leads unerringly all the way back to the start, a super stride across these purple acres.*

Features of interest en route are the Iron age Cross Dike, which is met at right-angles to our track. This is prominent even to the most unobservant walker, being well gouged and decorated with bracken. Just past it, the regularly dry Seavy Pool is passed in a small depression. Up the brow beyond, a notice advises of the presence of Bronze age barrows: these are clearly visible just across to the left, as pronounced mounds in the heather. They are reckoned to be between 3000 to 4000 years old, and the burial sites of families of tribal chiefs.

In these latter stages along the crest of the moor, we finally enjoy magnificent views down into the Hole of Horcum itself, a fitting conclusion. *At the end, a gate and stile take us off the moor, and so back to the top of Saltergate Bank.*

The Hole of Horcum

63

15

LEVISHAM MOOR

START Levisham Station   Grid ref. SE 818910

DISTANCE 5 miles

ORDNANCE SURVEY MAPS
1:50,000
Landranger 94 - Whitby *or*
              100 - Malton & Pickering
1:25,000
Outdoor Leisure 27 - North York Moors (East)

ACCESS Start from the station on the North Yorkshire Moors Railway, preferably having arrived on the steam train. Other than the station's own car park, there is some parking across the level crossing. An alternative start is from the village centre. The station is also a starting point for the Newton Dale Forest Drive, which eventually re-emerges at Stape.

Levisham's lovingly restored railway station stands a good two miles from the village by road, though Newton-on-Rawcliffe, the line's nearest village, is only a half-mile distant on foot. In its isolated position on the floor of Newton Dale, it is one of only three stations on the 18 mile line between Grosmont and Pickering. Closed by British Railways in 1965, the line was rescued from oblivion by enthusiasts to create the North Yorkshire Moors Railway. The sight of steam on this impressive route is a marvellous spectacle, and one that, with luck, can be enjoyed on reaching the moor-edge at its highest point.

❑ *The walk begins by starting up the road to Levisham, but almost immediately taking a gate into the woods on the right. From it a path rises through the trees to emerge into a field. At the top a stile gives access to a track which forks just to the right. Take the embanked green pathway which resembles an inclined tramway as it slants delectably up to a seat.*

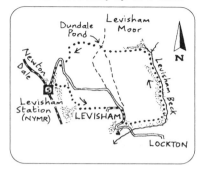

After a welcome sit to appraise the Newton Dale scene - where it will be appreciated there are great sweeps of real trees in evidence - **take the right-hand, lower path. This contours round the head of Keldgate Slack to a stile on the left at the far end. From it follow the field-sides, with the red roofs of Levisham appearing before joining a back lane to enter the village.**

Levisham is a good example of a 'street' village, its attractive stone dwellings stood well back from the road, with wide grassy margins. At the head of the street stands the Horseshoe inn, in front of which is a small green with a maypole. Also here is the church of St. John the Baptist, dating from 1884. The village stands on the edge of a broad plateau, the only access by road being from Lockton via the steep drop to - and back up from - Levisham Mill.

Levisham has as many man-made features of interest out of the village as within it. The walk already takes in the railway station in Newton Dale, but Levisham's own valley also has much to offer. The first item is the church of St. Mary, a former parish church which dates from the 11th century but was made new as recently as the 19th. Today it is but a shell, being steadily engulfed by undergrowth - maybe one day it will be restored again. It can be seen from the main path after leaving Levisham.

At Levisham Station

NORTH EASTERN RAILWAY
PUBLIC WARNING
PERSONS ARE WARNED NOT TO TRESPASS
ON THIS RAILWAY, OR ON ANY OF THE
LINES, STATIONS, WORKS, OR PREMISES
CONNECTED THEREWITH.
ANY PERSON SO TRESPASSING IS LIABLE
TO A PENALTY OF FORTY SHILLINGS.

SECRETARY.

65

St. Mary's, Levisham

Only 350 yards further upstream from the old church is another building which has lost its true vocation, for there are now holiday cottages at the former mill. It remains, however, a highly attractive scene, with ducks splashing by the beck, and a rusting waterwheel in situ.

Leave the village by the road to Lockton, but as it leaves the houses to drop through the woods take a narrow path heading away from the seat on the left. It remains narrow but clear as it undulates along the top of the steep bracken slope: at an early stage be sure to keep left to remain at the top, for an inviting arm at a waymarked fork tempts one to descend.

At a sharp corner our upper path swings left to run along Levisham Brow, high above Levisham Beck. *After departing the Hole of Horcum (see WALK 14) the beck flows through a steep-sided dale with slopes completely bracken covered. This little side valley is a real gem, especially in the glow of autumn, and the excellent path complements it. Whilst we might be in wild country, the valley is in reality sandwiched between some highly productive agricultural plateaux.*

The path eventually slants down a little before a fuller descent to an intervening gate. Just beyond is a guidepost by the beck. Here turn sharp left to follow a green path up the side of Dundale Griff,

a mini-dale that is more than likely to be dry. As height is gained, heather takes over from bracken, while sturdy oaks line the edge of the little ravine. A griff, incidentally, is a very localised word for a small side-valley.

At the moor top take the narrower right fork which runs gently along to Dundale Pond. The pond is an artificial sheet of water, thought to have been the work of the monks of Malton Priory in the 13th century, to cater for their flocks and herds which grazed here. This reed-fringed pool stands at a busy junction of moorland tracks, and is a regular host to rucksack picnics.

From the junction of paths here, either continue on past the pond to a wall corner, or (for better views) take the path rising half left to a wall, and then turn right to the wall-corner. Now follow this wall away to its next corner, then leave it by tracing a prominent mound to the edge of a steep drop. Below is the deep trough of Newton Dale with its well wooded slopes (see also WALK 13) and the road down to the station highly prominent. **A path then descends to the road to the station, cutting a corner of the sharp bend and rejoining the road to reach the bottom of the hill.**

Levisham Station

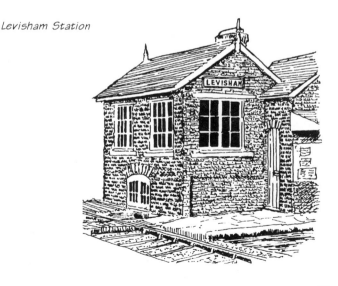

16

THORNTON DALE

START   Thornton Dale   Grid ref. SE 834830

DISTANCE   6 miles

ORDNANCE SURVEY MAPS
1:50,000
Landranger 100 - Malton & Pickering
1:25,000
Outdoor Leisure 27 - North York Moors (East)

ACCESS   Start from the cross in the village centre. There
is a large car central car park. Thornton Dale is served by
Scarborough-Pickering buses.

*Thornton Dale vies with Hutton-le-Hole for the attention of the
crowds, but has the disadvantage of being astride a busy highway.
Its Sunday name Thornton-le-Dale has all but disappeared, some-
thing its stream never does: what gives this village its real charm
is the way Thornton Beck glides through its centre, creating some
delightful corners.*

*Thornton has history too, with the church dating from the 14th
century (though much restored in 1866), the hall originally from
Tudor times and a row of almshouses and a former grammar school
from the mid-17th century. A 600-year old market cross and village
stocks complete things. Thornton Dale has shops, cafes and inns
to cope with its hefty passing trade.*

❑ *From the village centre take the main road towards Pickering,
and leave it at the brow of the hill (care is required crossing from
the footpath to the north side of the road) by a hidden footpath at
a stile just beyond a lane rising away. The ensuing fields offer far-
reaching views across the Vale of Pickering to the Wolds. **Cross to
the field corner and maintain the direction across the next field,***

then cross straight over the next two before clinging to the top of the last field before entering a wood. A path then heads down to a gate to the drive at Hagg House Farm.

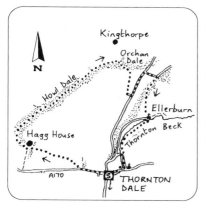

*Turn left over the cattle-grid and then leave by the first gate on the right. Follow the fence away to a stile into some trees, a path then materialising to swing down to the right to commence the long journey up wooded **Howl Dale.** This narrow, dry limestone valley is typical of many on the southern edge of the moors. Heavily wooded, its good mixture of trees gives splendid autumn colours in its woodland glades.*

The path clings to the floor of this narrow valley for well over a mile, with one major junction as a track comes in from the left. As the ground on the left steepens on the edge of the wood, turn up to a stile on the left, to resume the journey on the outside of the trees along the field bottom.

Thornton Beck at Thornton Dale

69

This neighbourhood is an important site for plants favouring limestone soils, and at the time of research this area was open to access under the Countryside Stewardship scheme, with signs around to acknowledge this. **Remain with the fence to the field corner, where a stile will be found pointing unconvincingly into an area of scrub.**

St. Hilda's, Ellerburn

A vague path heads away to join a better one in a clearing, turning left to immediately meet a wide track in Orchan Dale. Turn right up this to soon leave the trees and eventually empty onto a road. Head left to the first junction, then right towards the Dalby Forest drive. Our path goes off right, just before a broader track on a bend. It descends through woodland plastered with 'private' signs. Part-way it meets a wider path to soon leave the trees, descending a field-edge to emerge alongside the church at Ellerburn.

Ellerburn is a farming hamlet hidden from the outside world in the upper valley of Thornton Beck. A sign of the times is the trout hatchery where mills once operated, but the highlight is the tiny church of St. Hilda. It dates in part from Saxon times, and has carved crosses from the 10th and 11th centuries.

From the church cross straight over the bridge into the yard of Low Farm. Keeping right of all the buildings, a short path runs along to the right to a stile into a field. Adjacent to the burbling stream, this is a lovely spot. Head to the far left corner, and from the stile cross a cornfield to the next stile. Here turn down to the beck, tracing it downstream to enter a wooded corner. Here the path bears away from the beck to a works yard. Go ahead, passing the former feed mill.

This immense and impressive structure was still producing animal feeds at the first edition of this book, but sadly now it is merely a 'development opportunity'. **In this attractive location the road from Ellerburn is joined. Head away with a stream alongside:** Thornton Beck begins life as Staindale Beck in Dalby Forest. **Passing numerous private bridges, look out for the public one that provides a dream finish through a chocolate box scene.**

The old feed mill, Thornton Dale

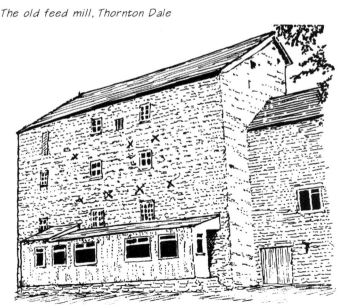

17

BRIDE STONES

START   Low Staindale   Grid ref. SE 877904

DISTANCE   5½ miles

ORDNANCE SURVEY MAPS
1:50,000
Landranger 94 - Whitby *or*
               101 - Scarborough & Bridlington
1:25,000
Outdoor Leisure 27 - North York Moors (East)

ACCESS   Start from the Low Staindale car parks, 3 miles
north of Low Dalby on the Forest Drive (toll payable) through
Dalby Forest. A toilet block helps confirm the location.

*Low Dalby is a Forestry Commission village with a visitor centre,
which makes a worthwhile stopping point en route to the start of
the walk. It is open from Easter to the end of October, 11.00 to
5.00. The Commission's policy is to encourage public usage, from
the Forest Drive to innumerable trails. The centre has leaflets and
various other publications on sale. Dalby Forest is a popular stage
on motoring rallies, though it is advisable for normal visitors to take
the Forest Drive a little more leisurely.*

*Much of this walk makes use of National Trust and Forestry
Commission permissive paths. A Bridestones Nature Trail has been
established, with an informative leaflet available.*

❑ **Start by heading towards the toilets, then drop down to the
beckside. A grassy path heads upstream by a picnic site to reach
the dam of Staindale Lake.** *The lake is artificial but nevertheless,
with its birdlife, very pleasant.* **Go left along the dam to the
roadside, then follow the shoreline path up to High Staindale car**

park, with its bird spotter and feeding station. Cross to the hairpin bend of the road, then straight over and along a forest road between houses. The blue indicators serve to identify our route as far as Crosscliff.

Ignoring an immediate branch right, this heads pleasantly away through the broad valley of Grain Beck, eventually arriving at a broad clearing where it swings sharp right. Here take the thinner way slanting up to the left: this rapidly narrows into a superb footpath, which winds its way up the narrowing Dargate Slack in delightfully colourful surrounds. At the top it meets a forest track, but simply continue straight over.

Through a more traditional plantation the path runs, crossing another track and now accompanying the pronounced ditch of Dargate Dikes, ancient earthworks. A firmer path comes in from the Crosscliff viewpoint car park over to the right, but how much more satisfying to approach it this way! A broad forest track is crossed just short of reaching the viewpoint. Here is a seat and informative view indicator.

While emergence from the trees is always a moment of rejoicing, this is particularly impressive for the scene presented is a marvellous combination of North York Moors scenery. Over to the right are the vast plantations of Dalby/Langdale Forest, beneath is the valley of Crosscliff Beck, ahead is a fine sweep of heather moorland, while working along to the left we have the Fylingdales RAF base, the island dome of Blakey Topping, and Hazelhead Moor and Newgate Brow (all features of WALK 18).

On leaving turn left along the broad forest track, which runs an unswerving course along Crosscliff Brow. Gaps in the trees offer regular views out to the environs of Blakey Topping, which itself becomes far more impressive now it breaks the skyline. Several ways branch off to the left, including, at last, the trusty blue trail. This edge track remains our way almost to the end of the wood.

73

The point of departure comes during a scruffy felled area on the left. A four-way guidepost by the track, with an old gatepost just to the right, indicates a crossroads of public footpaths. Our way is left. Through the tangle of debris a thin path has been forged, and within a minute we emerge at the other side onto Bridestones Moor. What a contrast! Wide open spaces and delectable heather moorland.

Turn left along the broad, inviting green trackway, descending ever gradually and affording time to savour the surroundings. On reaching a shallow depression with a handful of trees, take an initially slender path branching off to the right just after the trees and a slightly earlier track. This works through the heather keeping to the left of the forming Bridestones Griff. The views now unfold rapidly over Bride Stones country, and the High Bride Stones soon appear across to the right. Our thin path runs on to reveal the Low Bride Stones only at the last minute, and quickly then joins the main path around the stones.

Of the several bride stones scattered about the North York Moors, these are the best known. The two groupings of distinctive rocks have been created by natural weather erosion of their Jurassic sandstone, and these weird sculptures are further enhanced by their setting on the bracken covered Bridestones Moor. From the stones it will be noticed that the moor is but an island surrounded by forestry (north and east) and farmland (south and west).

The moor is owned by the National Trust and run jointly with the Yorkshire Naturalists' Trust. 300 acres were acquired in 1944, and a nature reserve established in 1966. A National Trust warden was appointed in 1987.

Looking north from Crosscliff viewpoint

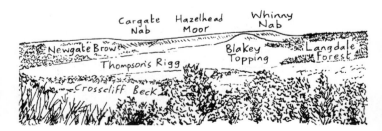

The best policy is to turn left along the path, and go as far as desired to visit the Low Bride Stones: certainly at least as far as the one depicted below and on the cover. Then re-trace steps around to the High Bride Stones. At the third of these the path turns sharp left, but a short detour right is recommended until the rocks expire. Some of these here are the most substantial outcrops, being also more firmly attached to their foundations. Back on the main path it now descends a modest spur, a fine promenade for appraising the line of Low Bride Stones over to the left.

A steeper descent of the end is made on a pitched footpath. This was being extended during my latest visit, a necessary result of the impact of vast visitor numbers. At the bottom is a footbridge over a stream, and a final view back up to our favourite Bride Stone on the skyline, before running through a long pasture to a footbridge back over the beck. Just beyond is a stile, and from it turn left to run along the top of several fields to return to a stile at the foot of the direct path onto the moor. The car park is just a minute or two further.

At Low Bride Stones

18

MALO CROSS

START Saltergate   Grid ref. SE 852937

DISTANCE 4¼ miles

ORDNANCE SURVEY MAPS
1:50,000
Landranger 94 - Whitby
1:25,000
Outdoor Leisure 27 - North York Moors (East)

ACCESS Start from the large car park above Saltergate Bank on the A169, half a mile south of the inn. Pickering-Whitby buses run along this road.

Before commencing the walk in earnest - or on concluding it - be sure to cross the road to witness the dramatic view down into the Hole of Horcum (scene of WALK 14).

❑ *From the car park turn north along the road, just as far as a road to the right. This is the access road to the farm at Newgate Foot.* With a name like Old Wife's Way, it was clearly put to good use long before becoming surfaced. While striding along it Blakey Topping appears, looking highly distinctive but a little meek, being no higher than our viewpoint. *The road is cheerfully followed until it begins a steep descent. Here head straight on along a wide track past a National Trust sign. Pass through a gate and continue above the bank.*

At a forlorn gatepost opposite a stile, first stand on it to help appraise the Bride Stones sitting merrily on their heather pocket moor. As we turn, also note the replacement for the golf balls at RAF Fylingdales to the north. Now leave the track by doubling back a couple of yards to drop to a stile. This descent of Newgate Brow *takes advantage of a former limers' route from Lockton's quarries to farms around Whitby. **A thin path drops through the bracken slopes, keeping just above a fence. At the bottom the diverted path remains along the fence top to join the drive just above Newgate Foot Farm.***

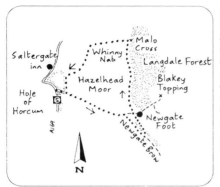

On arrival at Newgate Foot, Blakey Topping has gained a little superiority, now dominating the sky-line. This bracken-covered dome is a relic of the Ice Age, and is now largely surrounded by forestry. Its ascent makes a tempting detour, and an obvious one from Newgate Foot: though there is no right of way, it is under National Trust open access.

Cross to a stile opposite, and head away on a made green pathway. As it swings round, turn down to a gate, and head down the field to a stile by a gate. Now an old track runs outside the forest fence up the narrowing cleft between the steep bank and the forest. At a stile the bracken beneath Hazelhead Moor is entered, and a thin path fights its way through to a gate with Malo Cross just ahead. *A higher level option, though not the right of way, to the left uses a gate above the stile, and makes a far easier parallel green way through the bracken.*

Malo Cross stands at the foot of shapely Whinny Nab, a hill which it originally graced prior to being restored to its present site in modern times. It was a landmark on the old Whitby to Pickering road, and its prominent inscription is thought to refer to Richard Egerton, Knight.

Blakey Topping from Newgate Foot

*Malo Cross
and Whinny Nab*

Leaving the cross, take the path left alongside the fence beneath Whinny Nab. *Another non-right of way scales the Nab, then runs along its northern side as a thin trod to meet the rising footpath: it offers an outstanding prospect over the moorland to the north.* **Soon the lower path rises, broadening into a track on the moor. The broad green track runs on in grand style above Saltergate Brow,** *crossing the hugely prominent Double Dyke and revealing the white-walled inn below.*

Saltergate's name relates to it being astride an one-time salt traders' route. The inn has achieved a degree of prominence due to its peat fire that has reputedly burned for the best part of 200 years.

Eventually the track arrives at a wood. Here the right of way leaves the obvious track, going instead through the gate and then turning sharply left (a diverted route) between the parallel track along the moor-edge and the woodland. The slim path runs along to rejoin the farm road very near the start of the walk. Turn right to conclude the walk.

Saltergate and Levisham Moor from Double Dyke

19

LANGDALE RIGG

START   Langdale End   Grid ref. SE 939912

DISTANCE   5¼ miles

ORDNANCE SURVEY MAPS
1:50,000
Landranger 94 - Whitby *or*
          101 - Scarborough & Bridlington
1:25,000
Outdoor Leisure 27 - North York Moors (East)

ACCESS   Start from the centre of the hamlet, 2½ miles
west of Hackness. There is parking next to the phone box
below the pub, and also by the bridge at the bottom of the
hill. A very rare bus service operates from Scarborough.

*This is an exceptionally undemanding stroll through country
dominated, but not entirely choked, by the efforts of the Forestry
Commission.*

*Langdale End is an isolated farming hamlet. At its heart is the
Moorcock, a timeless country inn. Adjacent is the tiny Wesleyan
Methodist chapel, erected in 1822 and rebuilt in 1901. Down the
lane towards the bridge over the Derwent - a lovely corner in itself
- is the unassuming little church of St. Peter. Though deep in
forestry country, the hamlet is dominated by the modest little
Howden Hill, a bracken cloaked knoll.*

❏ **Head north along the road out of the hamlet, passing the last
farm (where honey might be obtained) and quickly reaching a fork.
The through road plunges downhill: here bear right along the level
Birch Hall Road.** *Shortly, a footpath sign indicates where our return
route will come back in. For now, remain on the traffic free road and
enjoy lovely views over this most peaceful corner of the district.*

The layout of the land hereabouts is intriguing. A range of rounded, largely wooded spurs project from the plateau across the dale, each incised by tiny side valleys: archetypal Tabular Hill country. Further ahead, up the valley, is the more saturated tree coverage of Langdale Forest, which gives preference to 'mountain bike' routes.

At another fork keep right, again on our contouring lane. The colourful bracken and birch covered slopes up to our right are the flanks of Langdale Rigg, along the crest of which our return is to be made. **Eventually the lane downgrades to a forest track on entering a plantation, though the early surrounds are currently largely felled. The same broad track, known as West Side Road (it has its own 'story'), runs on through the forest, never claustrophobic, and cushioned by bracken verges and a variety of fringe trees.**

Eventually a green pathway is met, slanting up from the left and continuing along to the right: the left branch carries the symbol of

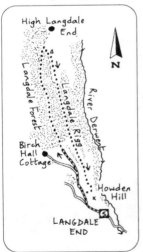

the 'blue man', a Forestry walking route, while that up to the right is marked as a mountain bike route. Take this green way, slanting gently up and curving round towards the end of the trees. Ahead is an open view towards the farmland of Harwood Dale, with a moorland skyline above. Up to the right, meanwhile, through diminishing trees, the rounded Langdale Rigg End itself is increasingly prominent.

A little short of a track junction, with open fields just ahead, there is a choice: a public footpath (poorly waymarked 'blue man' from this side) winds up into the trees to the rigg foot. A broad track climbs the edge of the plantation, rising across the slopes to the top. Here it leaves the track at a gate on the left. More interesting is a permissive option courtesy of Forest Enterprise: at the junction, with open fields in front, go right 50 or so yards to find a stile on the left. This admits to the base of the rounded end. Scale the slope to be deposited onto an ordinary field, oddly sited atop the afforested rigg. Just in front, Ordnance column S6331 sits innocently in the grass. There are good views now back over Harwood Dale, with the forest leading the eye to extensive Fylingdales Moor beyond.

Westwards, again beyond the forest, is the island dome of Blakey Topping, with Whinny Nab prominent to its right. **Leave by heading south along the field to use a gateway in an intervening fence. Here the direct footpath comes in from the forest road on the right.**

Together again, remain on the ridge top and head along the length of the pasture to a prominent ride in the plantation ahead. A stile admits to the plantation, and a broad track runs for a short mile through the length of the forest, the latter stage again recently felled. Emerging at the end the broad forest track is traded for a pathless sheep pasture, almost identical to that at the northern end. Again head straight on through this upland plateau, *largely unaware that to either side are steep, colourful bracken and scrub cloaked flanks. The views over the Langdale End environs are now super, despite the abundance of afforestation.*

Towards the end the slopes converge, and a distinct green path forms to wind down the nab end. *Ahead is the initially diminutive Howden Hill: though there is no access, a surprisingly clear path climbs to its little top.* **At the bottom of the rigg the path slants left and fades as the bracken ceases. Continue left down to a fence corner, and follow it along (on your right) to find a gate in a corner. Go right on a track the few yards to a stile by a gate,** *passing a notice deterring a detour onto Howden Hill.* **From the stile cross the field to another by a gate to rejoin Birch Hall Road. Go left for the final five minutes back to the start.**

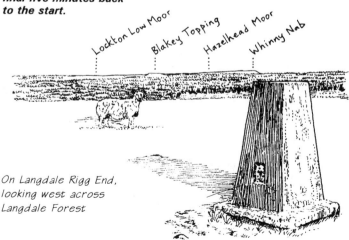

Lockton Low Moor   Blakey Topping   Hazelhead Moor   Whinny Nab

On Langdale Rigg End, looking west across Langdale Forest

20

FORGE VALLEY

START Ayton   Grid ref. SE 987847

DISTANCE   4 ½ miles

ORDNANCE SURVEY MAPS
1:50,000
Landranger 101 - Scarborough & Bridlington
1:25,000
Outdoor Leisure 27 - North York Moors (East)

ACCESS Start from the road bridge between East and West Ayton. There is parking by the hotel or the river in West Ayton. Scarborough-Pickering buses serve the village. An alternative start at the Green Gate car park at the halfway point gives the option of mid-walk refreshment in Ayton.

An easy walk through celebrated woodland.

The Forge Valley is the name given to a two mile length of the river Derwent as it forces its way south through a narrow break in the Tabular Hills. This escape into the Vale of Pickering was effected at the end of the last Ice age. The valley is so named because an iron foundry - possibly established by the monks of Rievaulx - existed here until the late 18th century: the forges were fuelled by charcoal made in these woods. The valley is a scene of wooded beauty in a corner of the park known more for its blanket of conifers. Of sufficient importance to be a National Nature Reserve, the valley bottom is filled by the untainted river and parallel road, and all else is rich slopes dominated by ash, oak and the like - a living relic of the wildwoods of ancient times.

Ayton is a bustling little spot, handily placed for Scarborough commuters but retaining its own independent character. The twin villages of East and West Ayton are divided by the Derwent, but linked by the long bridge that spans the river: this graceful four-arched structure was designed by the renowned John Carr of York, and dates from 1775. Each has a pub of its own, while interesting buildings in each community are the old mill and the church. West Ayton claims the former, which is passed at the very end of the walk, while East Ayton boasts the church of St. John the Baptist. Dating in part from the 13th century, it is a mellow old building that its innoccuous interior belies.

❑ **From the bridge turn towards East Ayton, leaving the main road after the Post office along Castlegate.** *Almost at once we have a* fine view over the Derwent to Ayton Castle, which will be passed at the end. **With its useful footway the road soon leaves the village, passing Ayton Lodge Hotel and dropping down to follow the river. Keep on past the first footpath sign by a nature reserve sign. Our route takes a steep path up through trees at the second footpath sign on the right, a little beyond a weir.**

At a fork just short of the top bear left. The path turns left to run along the top of the woods. *From the wall-side woodland delights are joined by views back to see the level plain backed by the long line of the Wolds.* **Just beyond Osborne Lodge Farm, the path drops back down into the woods.** *An early break in the trees reveals a splendid prospect out of the Forge Valley and further up the Derwent.* **At the bottom it merges with another path, then running on to the right to debouch into Green Gate car park.**

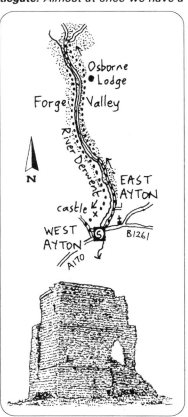

Ayton Castle

Turn left on the road to a junction and then left again. The 'Birdwatchers' car park is first passed before arriving at Old Man's Mouth car park. From here a short path runs to a wooden footbridge over the river, from where a well trodden path heads downstream. It clings to the water's edge as it glides serenely through glorious surrounds. A good deal of this is along boardwalks, intended to preserve the delicate habitat rather than our delicate feet. *At a second stile the river is forsaken as the path runs below the woods, rising to a gate to pass beneath the ruins of Ayton Castle.*

Ayton Castle was built as a fortified house by the Evers family in the 14th century, on the site of an earlier structure. Raised slightly above the village, it commands a wide view over the Vale of Pickering to the Wolds. It is very rare to find a pele tower such as this so far from the Scottish border, but the Scots did indeed raid the original structure on one of their forays south. Alongside is an extensive network of earthworks. *Just beyond, a short street is entered. Turn left at the end then left again on Mill Lane, to rejoin the Derwent at the impressive former mill.* This three-storey building is a splendid specimen, complementing a lovely corner where ducks waddle from the water to dabble on the broad grassy sward. *The main road is just yards downstream.*

Ayton Mill

21

DERWENT VALLEY

START Forge Valley   Grid ref. SE 984876

DISTANCE 5 ¾ miles

ORDNANCE SURVEY MAPS
1:50,000
Landranger 101 - Scarborough & Bridlington
1:25,000
Outdoor Leisure 27 - North York Moors (East)

ACCESS Start from the Hazel Head car park (and picnic site) near the edge of the woods at the northern end of the Forge Valley. A very infrequent bus service meets the route at Wrench Green.

Easy walking in a quiet corner, yet so near Scarborough. Autumn is a particularly rewarding time for a visit.

❑ *Turn right (south) out of the car park and follow the road past a junction. The 'Birdwatchers' car park is passed before reaching Old Man's Mouth car park. Enter this and take a path running the few yards to a footbridge over the Derwent. Turn to follow the river upstream, much of this initial section being on boardwalks.* These are here to protect the fragile environment rather than your feet, and in wet weather the wooden surface can be rather greasy. The surroundings, however, are delightful, and **the path remains with the swift and silent river until a stile out of the woods.**

Emerging into open pasture, head across the centre amid peaceful surrounds, with plantations and woodland decorating surrounding skylines. The winding river is regained at the end, and followed more faithfully now through several sheep pastures. Of interest is an embankment leading us away from the sluice where the Sea Cut is linked to the river. A glance at the Landranger map will show that logic dictates the river should flow east into the sea: it was the power of the last Ice age that caused the melting ice to force its way south to form the Forge Valley. This situation was remedied by Sir George Cayley of nearby Brompton in the early 19th century, who undid the work of the Ice age by cutting a channel to link the Derwent with the North Sea at Scalby Mills. It does, however, only divert excess water in order to prevent flooding, and the Derwent still flows a few dozen miles more to join the Ouse near Selby.

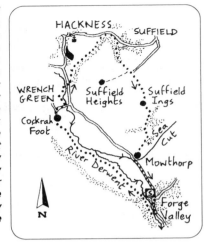

The way runs on along the loosely wooded base of a grassy slope to approach Cockrah House. Bear left to join a grassy drive just before the buildings, to descend through a gate to the yard and a surfaced road-end. Head out to a junction at Wrench Green and turn right, down to a bridge on the Derwent. After admiring the river and surrounds, don't cross but take a stile upstream, passing the small community of Wrench Green and tracing a flood embankment around to the sturdy Spa footbridge: a fine cameo finale by the Derwent. *This time cross the river to join the valley road.*

A few yards to the left is a stile. Climb the field behind and then bear left, above Mill Farm and beneath the woods to find a stile in an intervening fence. Advancing further, Hackness' splendid hall quickly comes into view. Hackness Hall dates from 1791, with an impressive west facing, seven-bay facade. It is the seat of Lord Derwent, and was restored after being ravaged by fire in 1910. The views here are altogether charming, looking over the lake with its swans and ducks; the church spire rising skywards from the trees; the green side valley of Low Dales striking off into a deep bowl of wooded slopes; and a general surround of wooded knolls on numerous skylines. *Remain close to the top of the pasture, just beneath the woods. After reaching the highest point directly above the hall, an inviting green path slants back down to a stile into the bottom of a wood. The path runs on to approach the road below, but is very reluctant to actually join it.*

86

Though strictly the path joins the road and follows it round into a clearing, a trod remains under the edge of the wood, curving round to slant back up to a gate and stile in a corner before the road climbs away at Cross Dales. Through this a thin path climbs through the undergrowth, tracing a small dry valley to its head. At the top an old limekiln is passed in a leafy glade. **The path runs on through the tapering woodland to emerge onto a broad track.** To the left are the scars of an old limestone quarry. **Bear along to the right to absorb the drive from Suffield Heights, and on to a junction with Limestone Lane. Turn right, following the road through the fields to Suffield Ings.**

Entering the yard, a small diversion sends us bearing left to a short enclosed way, past the house and then turning right to enter the field behind it. Head down the hedge-side to approach the top of a wooded bank. Just before entering the trees, note the surprise prospect of Scarborough Castle on its knoll high above the sea. **A path leaves this field corner to slant delightfully down through Hawthorn Wood.** It emerges with another fine view, over the Derwent Valley and our earlier steps.

Out of the trees, the path slants down the field top, affording a further glimpse over to a long seascape. After 100 yards or so the path turns to descend the well maintained route down the centre of this large field, joining a track at the corner of a wood. Go right to a stile by a gate to descend the grassy track to Mowthorpe Farm. Though the path presently bears right through its yard to emerge onto the valley road, watch for signs indicating a new diversion: the path will then avoid the farm by going further right to join the road. Go left over the bridge, where the Sea Cut is again in evidence. The last stage simply follows this road back to the car park, with a short-cut path leading back into a corner of the car park.

Derwent Valley from Mill Farm, Hackness

WHISPER DALES

START   Reasty Bank   Grid ref. SE 964943

DISTANCE   7 miles

ORDNANCE SURVEY MAPS
1:50,000
Landranger 94 - Whitby *or*
              101 - Scarborough & Bridlington
1:25,000
Outdoor Leisure 27 - North York Moors (East)

ACCESS   Start from the large Forestry Commission car parks at the top of Reasty Bank, above Harwood Dale on the road from Scalby. An alternative start is Hackness, where there is ample parking, on a quiet day, on the broad street near the church. Hackness has a very infrequent bus service from Scarborough.

The major feature of this walk is a long ramble through lovely Whisper Dales - whose wispish character lives up to its name - but the delectable Hackness is special in its own right, and the wooded edges of Reasty are also well worth the walk. All in all, this adds up to quite a stroll.

◻ *Having admired the prospect of Harwood Dale from the bank top viewpoint, cross to the western car park, behind which is a forest road parallel with the road. Branching off this is a hard forest road, setting off at a right-angle through the trees. Head away, and keep straight on where a branch forks right. Soon the way descends to the left, a very pleasant track that slants down to even pleasanter surrounds, the sudden arrival at the very head of Whisper Dales. So early in the walk, this is a superb moment, with rolling farmland locked between wooded banks. The track runs on to reach the farmhouse at Whisperdales.*

*Surprisingly, the solid track ends here, where one might have expected to meet the farm drive heading down the dale. **Keep on past the house on a grassy, field-side track with a tiny stream on the left.** In these lovely surrounds, remember to pause to appraise the scene behind as well as ahead. **The way crosses tiny Whisperdales Beck and continues as a better defined pathway, heading away to cross a field to a side-stream crossing before resuming as a broad green way.***

*The whole of this section is entirely delightful, being comprehensively enclosed by wooded slopes: a curious feature is that there is barely any sense of coming down a valley. The way remains level, the dale doesn't broaden, and the enclosing slopes never relent. It is also worth noting the not inconsiderable length of the walk through this dale, though certainly it is not a minute too long. **Eventually buildings are seen ahead. Passing a cottage the track becomes firm, quickly reaching a lovely corner at Lowdales, where the combination of ford and footbridge is duplicated within a few yards.***

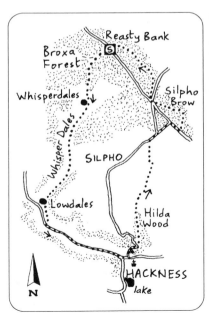

Just beyond, a surfaced lane takes over at the junction to High Dales. The lane can be avoided, initially, by taking a stile just along from the house on the left. A short lived field-path runs parallel to the lane for a couple of fields before joining it at a footbridge.

The final leg to Hackness is now along this very narrow and traffic free lane.** This long mile is barely inferior to those preceding, such is the unchanging quality of the surroundings. **The road is joined in Hackness with the church and its environs just along to the left.

Hackness is a gem of a place, a lovely village in a setting to match. The hustle and bustle of nearby Scarborough could be a hundred miles away. This a virtual estate village based on the magnificent hall, which is tucked away just further along the road east. It is, in fact, best viewed from the hillside to the south, on WALK 21. Hackness Hall dates from 1791, with an impressive west facing, seven-bay facade. It is the seat of Lord Derwent, and was restored after being ravaged by fire in 1910.

St. Peter's church is an imposing building, its tall spire prominent from many locations around the valley. Dating from the 11th century, though much changed down the years, the church is on the site of an earlier nunnery. Immediately on entering, you are greeted by the remains of an early Anglo-Saxon cross, dating from AD1050. Adjacent to the church is the village Post office and store, and also the little school. Further west along the road, past the wood fringed lake, are the bulk of the cottages that make up the other 'half' of Hackness.

On leaving, head up the narrow lane to Silpho, opposite the school. This quickly zigzags up the steep wooded bank. Part way up at a sharp bend left, take a stile by a gate on the right. A good footpath heads away through the mixed tree cover of Hilda Wood. Towards the top the trees are left behind, as we finish through sheep pasture at the dry head of this small side valley. At the very end is a stile at a crossroads of paths. Don't cross it, but turn up the fence side into the corner of a field. Continue a short way, then take a stile in the fence and head away with the crumbling vestiges of a wall. Several fields are crossed until the wall finally packs in. Now turn left as directed to the near field corner, turning right to follow the hedge alongside two fields to emerge onto a road.

Turn right along this road to soon reach a fork at the edge of the woods. Halt here and look into the first trees on the left to see a distinct sunken way: the same is noted on the right, between the fields. This overgrown hollow is Thieves Dyke, an ancient earth-work. Resuming, a corner can be cut here by taking the left branch through the trees to a junction with the 'main' road. Otherwise, **keep on the straight road to a T-junction at the bizzarely named Turkey Carpet picnic place, merely a grassy area.**

Turn right for 200 yards on the parallel, broad green way, then slip into the trees at a bridleway sign. Within yards a crossroads of green ways is met. Take the inviting one left, a footpath that unfortunately takes its share of horses. This runs pleasantly on,

*however, curving around **Silpho Brow**. At breaks in the trees it earns views over the long coastline of the North Sea. Part-way along, the imposing keep of Scarborough Castle is revealed on its 200ft knoll. **The path swings back round to rejoin the road at a crossroads where the short-cut comes in.***

*Cross only the side road road descending to the right, then return to the pathway into the trees. Within 100 yards a fork is reached. The left branch runs parallel with the road to return to the car parks. The right branch also leads unfailingly to the car parks, a far nicer journey well away from the road. This waymarked forestry path (white arrow on green, part of the 'Thieves Dikes Walk') also sees use by horse riders. It is another super route however, as it curves around **Surgate Brow**. Despite being along the pronounced edge of the hills, tree cover is such that there are few opportunities for distant prospects. There are, however, some glimpses over Harwood Dale, and the path is largely very good. **Eventually it emerges back at the viewpoint at the car parks.***

St. Peter's, Hackness

LOG OF THE WALKS

WALK	DATE	NOTES (companions, weather, wildlife etc)
1		
2		
3		
4		
5		
6		
7		
8		
9		
10		
11		

LOG OF THE WALKS

WALK	DATE	NOTES (companions, weather, wildlife etc)
12		
13		
14		
15		
16		
17		
18		
19		
20		
21		
22		

HILLSIDE GUIDES

■ *Circular Walks - Yorkshire Dales*

WHARFEDALE (Bolton Abbey to Buckden)
THREE PEAKS COUNTRY (Settle, Ingleton)
WENSLEYDALE (Hawes, Aysgarth, Middleham)
SWALEDALE (Keld, Muker, Reeth, Richmond)
HOWGILL FELLS (including Sedbergh)
NIDDERDALE (Pateley Bridge, Ramsgill, Fountains)
MALHAMDALE (Malham to Skipton, Upper Aire)

■ *Circular Walks - Peak District*

EASTERN PEAK (Stanage, Derwent Valley)
NORTHERN PEAK (Kinder Scout, Edale, Mam Tor)
CENTRAL PEAK (Bakewell, Eyam, Monsal Dale)
SOUTHERN PEAK (Dovedale, Matlock, Lathkill Dale)
WESTERN PEAK (Buxton, Roaches, Goyt Valley)

■ *Circular Walks - Lake District*

LAKELAND FELLS - AMBLESIDE & SOUTH
LAKELAND FELLS - PATTERDALE & EAST
LAKELAND FELLS - KESWICK & NORTH
LAKELAND FELLS - BUTTERMERE & WEST

■ *Circular Walks - South Pennines*

BRONTE COUNTRY (Haworth, Worth Valley)
CALDERDALE (around Hebden Bridge)
ILKLEY MOOR (includes Washburn Valley)
SOUTHERN PENNINES (Holmfirth, Saddleworth)

■ *Circular Walks - Lancashire*

BOWLAND (AONB of unspoilt moorland and villages)
PENDLE & the RIBBLE (Ribble Valley, Pendle Hill)
WEST PENNINE MOORS (Winter Hill, Darwen Moor)

■ *Circular Walks - North Pennines*

TEESDALE (High Force, Middleton, Barnard Castle)
EDEN VALLEY (Appleby, Kirkby Stephen, High Cup)

ACROSS THE NORTH

■ *Long Distance Walks*

COAST TO COAST WALK (the all-time classic)
DALES WAY (84 miles, Ilkley to Windermere)
CLEVELAND WAY (112 miles, Helmsley to Filey)
LADY ANNE'S WAY (100 miles, Skipton to Penrith)
WESTMORLAND WAY (95 miles, Appleby to Arnside)
FURNESS WAY (75 miles, Arnside to Ravenglass)
TRANS-PENNINE WAY (100 miles, Garstang to Ripon)
NIDDERDALE WAY (53 mile circular, Yorkshire Dales)
BRONTE WAY (45 miles, South Pennines)
CALDERDALE WAY (50 mile circular, South Pennines)
PENDLE WAY (45 mile circular, East Lancashire)

■ *Circular Walks - North York Moors*

WESTERN MOORS (Cleveland & Hambleton Hills)
SOUTHERN MOORS (Rosedale, Farndale, Forge Valley)

■ *Uplands of Britain (Hardback, Full colour)*

THE HIGH PEAKS OF ENGLAND & WALES
(walks on the 2500ft hills from Scafell Pike to Snowdon)
YORKSHIRE DALES, MOORS & FELLS
(walks in the broad acres from Penyghent to Swaledale)

■ *Waymaster Short Scenic Walks*

ESKDALE (North York Moors)
WHARFEDALE (Yorkshire Dales)
AMBLESIDE & LANGDALE (Lake District)

■ *Waymaster Visitor Guides*

YORKSHIRE DALES (a comprehensive guide)

■ *Biking Guides - Yorkshire*

YORKSHIRE DALES CYCLE WAY (130 mile road route)
AIRE VALLEY BIKING GUIDE (6 off-road routes)
CALDERDALE BIKING GUIDE (6 off-road routes)
WHARFEDALE BIKING GUIDE (6 off-road routes)

INDEX

Principal features: walk number refers